GW00320449

travel in health

A GUIDE TO HEALTHY TRAVELLING OVERSEAS

DR. GRAHAM FRY & VINCENT KENNY

bIOGRAPHIES

Dr. Graham Fry is a surgeon who specialises in tropical medicine. He first visited Africa in 1975, later living in Zaire with his wife and two children. Since his return to Ireland, his clinical practice is exclusively in tropical medicine and he sees many patients before their travels or after they return. He also has many lecturing commitments in tropical and travel medicine throughout the year and was instrumental in setting up the Tropical Medical Bureau in Dublin in 1988. He is married to Sylvia and has four children; Susan, Deborah, Peter and Laura.

Vincent Kenny is director of Community Health International, an Irish-based relief and development organisation. He has worked in Asia, South America and Africa. His wide experience of both rural and urban areas has given him a great understanding of the mechanisms of disease transmission and the means of their prevention. He is married to Terri and has four children; Damien, Brian, John and Jessica.

Editor **Vanessa Harriss** is a journalist and has worked with Eireann Publications, publisher of medical journals, since July 1995.

Richard Butler has worked as a freelance illustrator for ten years and his work has appeared in books, magazines and on film.

travel in health

◆

A GUIDE TO HEALTHY
TRAVELLING OVERSEAS

◆

Dr. Graham Fry &
Vincent Kenny

This publication has been co-sponsored by an educational grant from:
SmithKline Beecham Pharmaceuticals
Leading The Way In Vaccines

travel in health Contents

travel
in
health

♦

Published by Eireann Publications Limited,
28 South William Street, Dublin 2. 1996

"To boldly go where no man has ever gone, to search out new civilisations".

*t*here is little doubt that 20th century earthlings are travelling in a way that our forefathers would have regarded with utter amazement. We have the opportunity to see, to experience and to explore regions of our world that only a few travellers would have touched in past generations. This new-found ability to travel the world brings with it many pleasures, but also some dangers which may not always be self-evident.

New countries, and even regions within countries, may present risks to the traveller's health which need to be considered and dealt with appropriately. When we return from our travels we may carry with us, not only memories of visits to distant places, but also some unwanted visitors in the form of intestinal or blood parasites. These may not cause symptoms until weeks or even months after we return.

The range of illness to which we may find ourselves subjected varies from mild influenza to more severe life-threatening diseases. The major illnesses of the world have names most people have never heard of, such as trypanosomiasis, leishmaniasis and schistosomiasis; as well as the better-known malaria. These diseases, and many more, kill millions of people each year but don't despair. We can help you protect yourself from these and many more.

Unfortunately, even mild diseases can be significant on holiday, when suddenly you find yourself sick and stuck in the smallest room in the hotel. Was all the saving worth it? Of course it was, but first you must learn some basic rules and realise that staying healthy while abroad means following some common-sense rules ALL the time. Where and what to eat and drink; when to use sun blocking lotions and

how to avoid bites and stings from snakes, scorpions, insects or dogs. These are some of the basic simple guidelines for staying healthy while abroad.

The following chapters aim to cover the common pitfalls into which travellers can fall while overseas. Of course, this short book cannot be all-inclusive, but it does seek to cover the major causes of illness for the short term traveller. Whether you plan a sun-soaking holiday in southern Europe, a trekking tour through Africa or a business trip to Asia, illness can strike and upset even the best-laid plans. Don't ever think of yourself as a superhuman who can take chances with your most precious gift — your health.

So how can we describe the joys of foreign travel and yet still warn of the real risks to health which exist for the unwary?

Should we describe the world region by region in terms of disease? No, for this would not only alarm but also give a misleading impression of the beauty and happiness which most people experience on their foreign holiday. Also, the major cities of the world, whether they are in Asia, Africa, Europe or the Americas, are all fairly similar despite their cultural and climatic differences.

Wherever the tourist is in the world, he or she may find difficulty in relating to the new environment in so far as food, drink, temperature and culture are concerned. That is where this book will help. One of the problems with the idea of a 'holiday' is that you immediately relax; that is the idea, after all. But relaxing your body should not mean forgetting about risks. Follow us on a journey through some of the common health pitfalls, see how to

avoid them and experience the real joys of travelling in health.

The evolution of the information superhighway over the past few years has meant that travellers now have superb access to health information. Travellers can get the latest news on health risks, obtain up-to-date information on disease outbreaks and get general information on the necessary vaccinations for their journey. All of this information needs to be accessed with care — don't forget that training for medicine takes more than a few hours surfing the Net!

The Tropical Medical Bureau in Dublin has its own home page at http://www.iol.ie/~tmb. Visitors to the page can obtain printouts about malaria and avoiding insect bites while abroad. An e-mail facility is also available at <tropical@iol.ie>.

travel in health

—

Section 1

Before You Leave

G READY

GETTING

*h*aving decided to go on holiday, you need to organise yourself. Plan the build-up to your departure so that everything will run smoothly and there will be as few last minute hitches as possible.

Choosing the destination

Knowing what you want from the holiday is all important. Some travellers delight in an energetic holiday; others just want to flop down beside the sea and enjoy doing nothing. Make a decision and then discuss the possibilities with the travel agent. Don't forget, many of the better travel agencies will have sent employees to visit the destinations and so they will be able to give you an up-to-date run-down on the hotels and amenities.

Tell the travel agent of any special requirements you may have, ask their advice and listen to what they say. If you have arthritis, don't end up with a room on the fifth floor in a lift-less hotel. If you love swimming, don't find yourself miles from the beach in a hotel without a swimming pool.

Make a list of what you want in your destination. Mark the essential items and others which would be nice but you could live without.

- If you are planning an apartment holiday, ask how far the nearest shops are from the site

- Check if your hotel is miles away from the nearest town, and what the cost would be to hire a taxi

- If you have arthritis or a heart condition check if the region is very hilly and how many steps there are up to the hotel

- If you are in a wheelchair,

find out if there are easy access points and other facilities

Spending a few minutes asking these pertinent questions will help you to enjoy your holiday much more.

Visa and vaccination requirements

Again your travel agent will be able to help you here. Often a holiday visa is available at the point of entry. Phone or write to the embassy or consulate and make certain that the duration of your journey does not push you out of the 'holiday' visa category.

Details regarding vaccination advice are available from your local travel vaccination clinic. Travellers often ask what vaccinations are essential for their holiday. Frequently there will be no essential vaccines but some will be recommended for personal protection. The vaccination advice will be linked with other information regarding food- and water-borne disease, making the visit to the clinic very worthwhile. Know your itinerary and make a list of the questions you would like to have answered. If you are particularly prone to illness, or severe allergic reactions, ask for the names of English-speaking doctors in the area you plan to visit.

Where necessary, vaccinations will usually be given on two occasions before your trip. Try to plan the first visit at least four weeks before you leave if you are off on a short holiday. If you are planning a longer trip, organise yourself eight to 12 weeks ahead of your departure.

First aid kit

Travellers should throw together some kind of medical kit, even for the shortest trip overseas. Travel may bring certain risks and also, perhaps, the necessity to deal with emergency situations as they arise. Usually if there is a medical problem a few simple pain-killers will ease the situation. A few paracetamol may be all that is required for toothache, sunburn or a twisted ankle.

The following list contains many of the items necessary for the long-term traveller or for those planning a trekking holiday. Most short-term travellers will only require a very limited selection. The actual nature of the kit will also depend on your destination, the length of time you will be abroad and the activities in which you hope to engage. But remember, just because you have a first aid kit don't take on too much. If the situation is serious, look for qualified medical attention.

What to include in your first aid kit

- Thermometer
* Scissors
* Crepe bandages
- Sticking plasters

* Lint
* Cotton wool balls
* Savlon
- Antiseptic ointment
* Savlon liquid
- Paracetamol
- Disprin
- Anti-diarrhoeal tablets
- Anti-nausea tablets
- Triangular bandage
* First aid book
* Oral rehydration salts
* Syringes
* Sutures/needles, etc.
* Alcohol swabs
* Sleeping tablets
* Antihistamine tablets
- Antihistamine cream
- Sun tan lotion
* Burn spray
- Insect repellent cream
- Insect repellent coils
- After-bite cream
- After-sun ointment

* Antibiotics
  - Tetracycline
  - Cotrimoxazole
  - Metronidazole
• Thrush preparation
* Anti-fungal ointment
• Dental repair kit
• Water purification tablets
* Water filter pump
* Eye ointment
* Steroid ointment
* Cold sore ointment
* Safety pins
* Tweezers
* Blood sampling bottles
* Non-adhesive dressings
* Wound dressings
* Anti-inflammatory ointment
* Calamine lotion
* Hypochlorite solution e.g. Domestos/Milton
* Malaria standby treatment

• Suggested for short-term travellers.

Medical check

For many travellers this will not be necessary. However, for others a trip to their doctor a month or so before they leave (perhaps even before they finally book and pay for their holiday) may be very worthwhile.

The main group of otherwise healthy travellers who will benefit from a medical check are those planning to go up very high and those planning to go down very low. (The risk of altitude sickness is outlined in a separate chapter.) Scuba diving is also becoming more popular and it is essential that travellers know that their ears are perfect before they dive. Any traveller with a history of ear problems or who is subject to panic attacks should really think twice before going down to any significant depth.

INTRODUCTION TO V

VACCINES

Introduction to vaccines

Most travellers fear vaccines. Nowadays, vaccines have greatly improved and modern techniques mean that fear of the visit to the vaccination centre is a thing of the past. Vaccination centres are designed to be user-friendly and hurting people is not good for business!

What are vaccines?

Sometimes, to protect you against a disease, the doctor may give you a small portion of the infection to help you build up your body's defences. These small doses of infection have been carefully selected so that they are not too strong for your system and yet are sufficient to create a good degree of protection.

How do they work?

Vaccines work by stimulating our immune system to form antibodies which are capable of fighting infectious agents. Some of the vaccines can be taken by mouth and others require an injection. The antibodies may need to be reinforced through the use of booster doses. The memory system within the body differs from vaccine to vaccine and so the booster doses are given at varying times, from months to many years.

Of course, not all diseases can

be stopped in this way but many can and the use of vaccines is a sensible precaution for the international traveller. Newer and safer vaccines are continually being developed, allowing travellers to visit remote areas of our world without many of the risks to which previous travellers were exposed.

Contraindications to vaccines

The majority of people can have vaccines without worry but there are a few special groups which require particular attention. You should tell the doctor before your vaccinations if any of the following apply to you:

- Pregnancy (either confirmed or possible)
- Breast feeding
- Eczema/Psoriasis

- Sarcoidosis/Addison's/ Diabetes
- Asthma/Epilepsy/AIDS
- On any medication
- Any drug allergy, e.g. to sulphonamides, penicillin, aspirin, etc.
- Any food allergy, e.g. to milk products, egg allergy, etc.
- Close contact with sick people, e.g. nurse, doctor, etc.

Side effects?

There are very few significant side-effects associated with the modern vaccines but look out for the following:

- Soreness and redness at the vaccine site (This was more commonly seen with the older typhoid and cholera vaccines It is uncommon today.)
- Stiffness in the shoulder on the same side
- Influenza symptoms
- Headache and skin rash (These are very rare but can occasionally occur.)

If you have any effect which you feel may be due to the vaccines, ring the doctor.

Essential or recommended?

Vaccinations may be compulsory for entry/exit purposes or merely recommended for personal protection. Vaccinations that are required for entry/exit purposes are generally used to halt the entry of disease into the country in question. When vaccinations are recommended for your own personal protection this often means that the country already has the disease and you should be protected against it.

When should you start your vaccines?

Vaccinations usually take time to work effectively. For most two-to three-week trips it is wise to attend for your initial vaccines and health brief about a month before your journey. If you plan to travel abroad for longer, then it may be wise to see the doctor two or three months before your departure date.

Which vaccines?

This will depend on various factors including your itinerary, your planned activities abroad and the duration of your stay.

For most holidays to a developing country the traveller will be advised to consider vaccination against poliomyelitis, typhoid, tetanus and hepatitis A. In some cases, vaccination

against yellow fever may also be required. Also, those planning a more adventurous trip, or those who are going to live abroad, should consider vaccination against some or all of the following: —

MENINGITIS A & C

RABIES

HEPATITIS B

JAPANESE B ENCEPHALITIS

DIPHTHERIA

There is no vaccine against malaria. Tablets are used instead and should be started a few days before exposure (see section 2, chapter 3). The actual schedule for your journey will need to be worked out carefully by the vaccination doctor. The doctor will be able to take into account your past medical history and the risk factors associated with your trip.

H

FOR TRAVELLING

*i*t will not be possible to cover every possible situation which might occur while you are abroad. It is, however, possible to give a brief list of hints which will be of assistance to some specific groups during their travels. If you are travelling while pregnant, travelling with children, or if you have diabetes, asthma or heart disease, you may feel that travel is practically forbidden to you.

Travelling under any of these circumstances can be frustrating and, indeed, occasionally dangerous. However, if you watch out for some of the more common pitfalls, you will be able to enjoy the holiday with some peace of mind.

Travelling while pregnant

Going on an overseas journey when you are expecting a baby can cause you a certain amount of anxiety. Is it safe to travel? Are there extra precautions which should be taken? What about the vaccines and the malaria tablets?

If this is your first pregnancy you must realise that you are travelling uncharted territory as far as you personally are concerned. In the majority of cases the pregnancy will progress easily with no serious difficulties. After all, pregnancy is a normal physiological event. Still, travelling during the first months especially may expose you and your unborn child to certain risks.

Pregnancy can be easily divided into three stages. During the first three months mothers are sometimes nauseated and travelling may make this more pronounced. During the final three months of the pregnancy the mother will be carrying a lot of extra weight. This makes exercise more tiring and also increased pressure on the bladder may mean more frequent trips to the loo. The final stage of pregnancy is not an ideal time to travel. Airlines are not that keen to have a potential delivery at 36,000 feet and in consequence they restrict air travel to the earlier part of pregnancy. In the middle stage most pregnant women are very well and if you have to travel this may be the most advisable time.

Where you plan to visit on your trip is also critically important with regard to safety while abroad. In many of the overseas holiday destinations there may be very few English-speaking doctors and it may be difficult to explain your symptoms if this becomes necessary.

During pregnancy the body diverts some of its blood supply to the womb and energy is required for the developing child. Pregnant travellers may tire more easily, even with very mild exercise. It is essential to maintain a good fluid intake and ensure that sensible rest periods are taken so that exhaustion does not occur. These travellers will also be more sensitive to temperature changes.

Immunisations and malaria prophylactic tablets may normally be recommended for the itinerary in question but the general rule for pregnancy is to avoid all medication where possible, at least during the first three months. If vaccines are normally recommended for your proposed journey then it is essential that you discuss the risks in detail with doctor. Usually doctors will shy away from using vaccines like polio and typhoid at all stages during pregnancy. However, gamma globulin is widely used to protect against infectious hepatitis.

Malaria tablets will be prescribed if you will be entering a malarial zone. The risk of not taking the medication may be greater to you and the baby than the small risk involved in taking the tablets. Usually chloroquine and proguanil are used and over the years they have been shown to be safe throughout pregnancy.

What has to be recognised is that there are special risks involved in travelling overseas while pregnant. It is difficult to give adequate vaccine cover and personal immunity against infections may be lowered. In most cases the risks to both the mother and the unborn child are too high unless the trip is essential.

Travelling with children

While it is certainly true that children can make a holiday, some of the most harrowing experiences abroad are associated with children falling ill, having an accident, getting lost or being bitten by an animal. If you are planning a trip with young children consider the following:

Is the destination suitable for children? 'Interesting' ruins are fine for a day or two but not for the entire holiday! If facilities are not provided for children then they tend to seek out their own entertainment. This may involve them wandering off by themselves. Always make sure the children know the name of the place where you are staying. Have a family plan in case someone goes missing. Warn your children never to wander off by themselves and never to befriend strangers. Another thing to remember is that exploration and children go hand in hand. Be extra vigilant when there are potentially dangerous caves, holes, cliffs and street alleys all waiting to be discovered.

Children have a habit of getting sick very quickly. Fortunately they also seem to recover at the same speed. However, one of the commonest problems on holiday is sunburn. A sunburnt child can make for a miserable holiday for you and the child. Use high factor blocking lotions and cover them up well. Children especially love to play outside in the early hours of dusk. This is usually the worst

time for mosquitoes and other nasty biting insects. Remember to make sure the whole family take their malaria tablets if recommended for the region.

Encourage your children to stay away from all animals during your holiday. The risk of rabies may be quite small but you really don't want to be searching around for a hospital to stitch any nasty bite.

Travelling with diabetes

With a condition like diabetes, a foreign journey may not seem worth the trouble and risk. Yet all it takes is a bit of common sense and the willingness to follow a few basic rules.

It is vital that your diabetes is stable. If you have been recently diagnosed then check with your physician before you book your trip overseas. The doctor may suggest that you wait until your condition is well controlled for your own safety. Firstly, check the availability of medical services in the area. Ask your travel vaccination centre for a list of English-speaking doctors, especially if you plan to go off the beaten track.

For your journey, carry all your own insulin, oral hypogly-caemics, syringes, needles, alcohol swabs and glucose monitoring devices you need for the length of time you plan to stay overseas. It is essential that you carry your own medications as preparations of insulin or hypo-glycaemic drugs may vary from country to country. Store your insulin in a small cool thermos flask for travelling and then place it, opened, in the lower part of the fridge as soon as you arrive. If there is no fridge in your bedroom ask your holiday representative. Remember that insulin will deteriorate if it is exposed to high temperatures so do not place it

in the boot of your car or the glove compartment.

Tell your tour operator about your diabetes. Make certain the information is passed on to your destination. This will help to make certain that the specific requirements of your diabetic diet will be available well in advance. Sometimes it can be very difficult to identify the calorie/sugar content of foods you have not tried before. Especially over the first few days, watch what you eat, and if you are unsure of the glucose content within your diet, monitor your glucose levels more often and adjust your intake to compensate.

Before you leave make sure you have a letter from your physician, on headed writing paper, outlining your requirements for insulin and the accompanying equipment. Keep all medications in their original containers.

Diabetic travellers may become hypoglycaemic very rapidly. This can be due to a combination of factors, such as different diet, irregular meals and more exercise. It is essential that your fellow travellers know what is happening so they can help. Always wear a medi-alert bracelet or carry a laminated information card.

When you travel across time zones it is easy to continue your medication but you may miss out on your regular meals. Know the number of time zones you will be travelling across. Travelling north to south will usually require no specific changes to your normal regime. If you are travelling east to west or from west to east across more than six time zones then you will need to make adjustments. How you should alter your medication will depend on the stability of your condition and you should always ask the advice of your physician before you travel. A good tip is to leave your watch set at 'home' time for at least the first 24 hours. This will help you to adjust your insulin dosage correctly. Always carry some glucose sweets on your person in case you feel yourself entering a hypoglycaemic phase. If you feel 'off-colour' don't delay in telling somebody so that they will be able to assist if necessary. Never fear travelling as a diabetic, just take care.

Travelling with asthma

Like diabetes, those suffering with asthma may also fear travelling. Again, the stability of your condition and the necessity of using medication frequently will play a large role in deciding whether or not to travel abroad. Asthma may occur spontaneously or in association with a specific stimulus. Patients with allergies

to hay, dust, insect bites or stings, dogs or cats etc. may go into an asthma attack very rapidly.

Of course, if you know what tends to set off an attack, it is easier to protect yourself. However, if you are quite unstable and have attacks frequently, then it is likely that you will suffer in any part of the world. Patients who use medication to treat themselves on a daily basis are regarded as unstable. Others are able to take tablets or sprays to protect against asthma and may not have

had an attack for weeks or even months.

Before you decide to travel, ask your doctor's advice. Know your itinerary and also if you plan to climb to altitude. Have a physical check-up and make sure you are in good shape. Remember that vaccines may set off an asthmatic attack, though this is rare. Check with your travel agent about the amount of pollution or dust in the region you hope to visit. Pollution levels may be so high during some seasons that asthmatic attacks may be initiated. Also, ask the tour operator about the facilities in the resort, the need for climbing steps or hills and the availability of English-speaking doctors. Carry enough medication for your trip with you on your person, not in your suitcase. Have a letter from your doctor outlining your needs to make sure you do not get stopped at custom check points.

During your holiday don't take on too much and always treat any wheeze as soon as possible to try and make sure it does not progress to a severe attack. If you have a significant allergy to stings and bites carry a small emergency kit and wear a medi-alert bracelet. Be careful while swimming and especially if you plan to scuba dive.

Travelling with heart disease

If you have decided to travel, you probably do not have very severe heart disease. More than likely you have a touch of angina or a degree of hypertension. A lot depends on your exercise potential. If you get puffed easily then going on an inter-continental holiday may really be too much. Just trying to get from here to there can be enough to wear you out.

Still, if you decide that you are definitely going, take care to make sure that you are not on the top floor in a hotel with no lift. Ask how many steps from the hotel lobby to the shops or beach. Check on the temperatures and humidity at the time you will be there. Be certain that you will not have to travel to altitude. This is especially important if you are just stopping off in a city like Quito, in Ecuador. Quito is at 9,350 feet and even though the rest of your holiday may be down on the coast, a short stop-over at such a high altitude is potentially very dangerous.

Carrying your medication on your person makes just as much sense for the traveller with heart disease as it does for the diabetic or asthmatic traveller. Have a letter from your physician, know the names of English-speaking doctors in the area and don't take on too much while you are abroad.

THE TRAVELLER'S CHECK LIST

*i*t is always wise to make out a check list coming up to any holiday. You may need to start the list a few months before you travel, especially if you require more extensive vaccinations than the standard two week holiday-maker.

There is no perfect check list. The items mentioned here are ones which, down through the years, have been found worthwhile. They are not in any particular order of importance, and they would depend on your actual itinerary.

Check out the travel agent. Only use a bonded travel agent. Ask your friends for their personal recommendations.

Travel insurance. Usually this is a very wise precaution for your journey. If you pay for your tickets on a major credit card there may be substantial travel insurance available.

Do you require a visa? As the international travel population continues to grow, we are now seeing that more countries are willing to issue visas at the point of entry. Nevertheless, do make certain that a visa is not required, or if it is, that it can be issued at the point of entry. This is particularly important with regard to entry into the United States.

Do you need a passport? Most times the answer will be yes. Even on short trips between some of the EU countries your passport is still required to prove that you do not need a passport! If you have children, make sure that they are on your passport.

When does your passport expire? Check it NOW. Some countries require you to have a good two or three months still valid on your passport beyond your proposed date of departure. Also, some countries will look carefully to see where you have visited before. Make sure there is no conflict.

Do you require any vaccinations? This can always be checked by telephoning your local travel vaccination centre. The general advice given will be that if your journey takes you beyond Western Europe, North America or Australia, you may have to consider the need for vaccination.

Are malaria tablets necessary? Once again, check this out with the local travel vaccination centre. In some countries the risk may be seasonal, i.e. during the rainy season or through the summer months, tablets may be necessary. If they are required, don't forget to take them for a few days before your exposure; during the time spent in the malarial zones and for at least another four full weeks after you leave the risk area.

Is sun tan lotion necessary? Bring a variety of blocking factors depending on your skin type.

Are insect repellents necessary? Where there are insects, you need repellents! Stick to the better quality ones which are known to work. If you have sensitive skin, make sure your skin is not allergic to the brand you choose by applying a small quantity on the back of your forearm a few weeks before your journey. Remember that some preparations can be corrosive to fabrics and plastics.

Have you local currency? In

many of the developing countries it is not possible to obtain their currency before you arrive. If this is the case, then take sterling or US dollars; a small quantity in cash and the rest in travellers cheques. Bring your credit cards if they are of use in the area you plan to visit. Some international dialling cards might be worth considering, depending on your destination.

Prescription for your glasses? If you have difficulty seeing without your glasses, or lenses, make sure that you have a spare pair with you and perhaps pack the script in case anything goes wrong.

Check your departure date and time. Many a traveller has been caught by not realising the actual flight date and time. Again, check it NOW. Remember how long it takes to reach the airport, especially at rush hour, and plan for any possible delays.

Are you normally on any medication? If you are on any medication for diabetes, epilepsy, asthma, blood pressure, the Pill or anything which you cannot do without, then pack a sufficient supply with you to carry on your person. Do not pack your entire supply in your suitcase in case of luggage mix-ups.

Pack a supply of 'holiday tablets'. While you are away from home, one of the most memorable times you may have is wishing you had packed a small quantity of tablets for nausea and the dreaded tummy bug. Just bring enough to get you past the main symptoms.

Contact names. If you plan to travel extensively, and especially off the beaten track, try and get the names of the major embassies and also some of the English-speaking doctors in the areas you hope to visit.

Leave your home organised. Cancel regular deliveries like

milk, papers, oil, coal etc. Inform your neighbours that you will be out of the house and ask them to keep an eye on the place in your absence. Inform your local police station. Finally, turn off electrical goods and empty the fridge of perishables. Unplug everything: all appliances and the television and radio aerials. Turn off the immersion heater and the boiler. Secure your house and valuables before you leave. Make sure that you only bring items which are not of great sentimental value. Hide your valuables well and don't forget that most of the 'better crooks' now use metal detectors to find your goodies more swiftly.

Make an itinerary. Make a detailed itinerary of your proposed journey and mark in possible contact points. Give dates, airline carriers, flight numbers, flight times, hotel/hostel addresses and telephone numbers. Make a few copies. Keep two yourself; pack one in your suitcase and keep the other handy with your passport and tickets. Give a copy to a responsible person at home just in case you need to be contacted while away.

Photocopies of essential documents. Before you leave make two photocopies of your passport and also your return air ticket. Leave one at home and pack the other separate from your normal documents. If you lose your passport or your tickets then at least you should be able to prove who you are and where you are supposed to be going.

Passport photographs. These are invaluable if you are planning a trekking holiday. Frequently at custom checkpoints you will be asked for a photo for some document or other. If you plan to cross borders bring plenty.

VOLTAGES
OF THE WORLD

If you plan to take any electrical appliances with you, bear in mind that the voltage varies from country to country.

Afghanistan	220v	Canada	110/120v
Albania	220v	Canary Is.	220v
Algeria	220v	Cayman Is.	110v
Angola	220v	Cent. African Rep.	220v
Argentina	220v	Chad	220v
Australia	240v	China	220v
Austria	220v	Colombia	110v
Azores	220v	Congo	220v
Bahamas	110/120v	Cook Is.	230v
Bahrain	240v	Corfu	220v
Bali	220v	Corsica	220v
Bangladesh	220v	Costa Rica	120v
Barbados	110/120v	Crete	220v
Belize	220v	Cuba	110/120v
Belgium	220v	Cyprus	240v
Benin Rep.	220v	Czech Rep.	220v
Bermuda	110/120v	Denmark	220v
Bhutan	230v	Djibouti	220v
Bolivia (La Paz)	110v	Dominican Rep.	110/120v
(elsewhere)	220v	East Timor	220v
Botswana	220v	Ecuador	110/120v
Brazil	110/120v	Egypt	220v
Britain	240v	El Salvador	110v
Brunei	220v	Ethiopia	220v
Bulgaria	220v	Falkland Is.	240v
Burkina Faso	220v	Fiji	240v
Burma (Myanmar)	220v	Finland	220v
Burundi	220v	France	220v
Cambodia	220v	French Guiana	120v
Cameroon	220v	Fr. Polynesia	110v

Gabon	220v	Majorca	220v
Gambia	200v	Malawi	240v
Germany	220v	Malaysia	220v
Ghana	220v	Maldives	220v
Gibraltar	240v	Mali	220v
Greece	220v	Malta	240v
Grenada	220v	Martinique	220v
Guatemala	110/120v	Mauritania	220v
Guinea Eq.	220v	Mauritius	240v
Guinea Bissau	220v	Mexico	110/120v
Guinea Rep.	220v	Minorca	220v
Guyana	110v	Monaco	220v
Haiti	110v	Mongolia	220v
Hawaii	110/120v	Morocco	220v
Honduras Rep.	110v	Mozambique	220v
Hong Kong	220v	Namibia	240v
Hungary	220v	Nepal	220v
Ibiza	220v	Netherlands	220v
Iceland	220v	Neth. Antilles	220v
India	220v	New Caledonia	220v
Indonesia	220v	New Zealand	230v
Iran	220v	Nicaragua	110/120v
Iraq	220v	Niger	220v
Ireland	240v	Nigeria	240v
Israel	220v	Norway	220v
Italy	220v	Oman	220v
Ivory Coast	220v	Pakistan	220v
Jamaica	110/120v	Panama	220v
Japan	110/120v	Papua New Guinea	240v
Jordan	220v	Paraguay	220v
Kenya	240v	Peru	220v
Korea	220v	Philippines	110/120v
Kuwait	240v	Poland	220v
Laos	220v	Portugal	220v
Lebanon	220v	Puerto Rico	110v
Lesotho	220v	Qatar	240v
Liberia	240v	Reunion	110v
Libya	125v	Romania	220v
Luxembourg	220v	Russia	220v
Madagascar	220v	Rwanda	220v
Madeira	220v	Samoa	220v

Sardinia	220v
Saudi Arabia	220v
Senegal	110v
Seychelles	240v
Sierra Leone	240v
Singapore	220v
Slovakia	220v
Solomon Is.	240v
Somalia	220v
South Africa	250v
Spain	220v
Sri Lanka	230v
St. Lucia	220v
Sudan	240v
Surinam	110v
Swaziland	240v
Sweden	220v
Switzerland	220v
Syria	220v
Taiwan	110/120v
Tanzania	240v
Thailand	220v
Tobago	110/120v
Togo	220v
Trinidad	110/120v
Tunisia	220v
Turkey	220v
Uganda	240v
United Arab Em.	220v
Uruguay	220v
USA	110/120v
Former USSR	220v
Vanuatu	220v
Venezuela	120v
Vietnam	220v
Yemen	220v
Yugoslavia	220v
Zaire	220v
Zambia	240v
Zimbabwe	240v

It is only when you begin to pack that you realise how dependent we have become on electrical gadgets. Electricity comes in two basic forms, Alternating Current (AC) and Direct Current (DC). Many portable appliances incorporate both systems, i.e. we can use batteries or the mains electric socket. Obviously the length of your overseas stay will dictate the number of batteries required. You will be amazed at just how universal the standard 1.5 volt AA type battery has become.

The other possibility is to check if an AC service is available. If there is, then the next question is what voltage is used in the area. Internationally there are two basic consumer voltage systems. The USA standard 110/120 and the European 220/240. In practical terms the voltage fluctuations within these two standards does not appear to affect the majority of modern electrical equipment. Check the official voltage for the country you will visit and purchase a transformer if necessary.

Despite the fact that all possible care has been taken to ensure that the figures mentioned above are correct, the authors cannot accept liability for any inaccuracies. If you require further information contact the appropriate embassy or consulate.

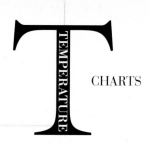

TEMPERATURE CHARTS

Average January and July temperatures in Fahrenheit.

	Jan	Jul
Alice Springs	83.5	53.0
Athens	48.0	81.0
Baghdad	49.5	93.0
Bahamas, Nassau	77.1	81.5
Beirut	56.5	80.0
Bombay	75.0	81.0
Buenos Aires	74.0	49.5
Cairo	56.0	83.0
Calcutta	67.5	84.0
Cape Town	69.0	54.0
Caracas	65.5	69.5
Chicago	25.0	73.5
Christchurch, N.Z.	61.5	42.5
Cologne	36.0	65.5
Colombo	79.0	81.0
Darwin	83.5	77.0
Delhi	57.0	88.5
Dublin	40.0	60.0
Funchal, Madeira	61.0	70.5

Geneva	34.0	67.5
Hamilton, Bermuda	63.0	79.0
Hong Kong	60.0	82.5
Istanbul	40.5	73.0
Jerusalem	48.0	75.0
Johannesburg	68.0	51.0
Lagos	81.0	78.5
Lima	74.0	62.0
Livingstone	75.5	61.0
London	39.5	64.0
Los Angeles	55.5	70.5
Majorca	49.5	75.0
Mexico City	54.0	63.0
Miami	67.5	82.0
Mombasa	81.0	76.0
Moscow	15.0	65.5
Nairobi	65.5	60.0
New York	30.5	74.0
Oslo	25.0	64.5
Paris	37.0	65.5
Rio de Janeiro	78.5	69.0
Rome	46.5	76.0
Singapore	79.5	81.5
Sydney	71.5	53.0
Tangier	53.5	72.0
Tokyo	38.0	76.5
Valparaiso, Chile	64.0	53.5
Winnipeg	-3.0	67.0

RAINFALL CHARTS

Average January and July rainfall in inches.

	Jan	Jul
Alice Springs	1.7	0.3
Athens	2.2	0.2
Baghdad	0.9	<0.1
Bahamas, Nassau	1.4	5.8
Beirut	7.5	<0.1
Bombay	0.1	24.3
Buenos Aires	3.1	2.2
Cairo	0.2	0.0
Calcutta	0.4	12.8
Cape Town	0.6	3.5
Caracas	0.9	4.3
Chicago	2.0	3.3
Christchurch, N.Z.	2.2	2.7
Cologne	2.0	3.2
Colombo	3.5	5.3
Darwin	15.2	<0.1
Delhi	0.9	7.1
Dublin	2.0	2.2
Funchal, Madeira	2.5	<0.1

Geneva	1.9	2.9
Hamilton, Bermuda	4.4	4.5
Hong Kong	1.3	15.0
Istanbul	3.7	1.7
Jerusalem	5.2	0.0
Johannesburg	4.5	0.3
Lagos	1.1	11.0
Lima	<0.1	0.3
Livingstone	5.7	0.0
London	2.0	2.0
Los Angeles	3.1	<0.1
Majorca	1.4	0.2
Mexico City	0.5	6.7
Miami	2.8	6.1
Mombasa	1.0	3.5
Moscow	1.5	3.0
Nairobi	1.5	0.6
New York	3.7	4.2
Oslo	1.7	2.9
Paris	1.5	2.1
Rio de Janeiro	4.9	1.6
Rome	2.7	0.6
Singapore	9.9	6.7
Sydney	3.5	4.6
Tangier	4.5	<0.1
Tokyo	1.9	5.6
Valparaiso, Chile	0.1	3.9
Winnipeg	0.9	3.1

YELLOW FEVER ENDEMIC COUNTRIES

*i*f a country is endemic for yellow fever it means that either transmission is known to occur at present or that the disease has been reported in the recent past. The incidence of yellow fever in travellers is extremely small but vaccination may be required for entry/exit purposes.

Yellow fever is a viral disease transmitted by the bite of an infected mosquito. The main spread of the disease is in Western Africa and parts of South America. Transmission has not been shown in Asia. This is despite the fact that the mosquito vectors occur and the climate is suitable. It is for this reason that some countries will insist on prior vaccination if a traveller has been through an endemic region.

The following countries may require visitors to have yellow fever vaccinations.

Angola
Benin Rep.
Bolivia
Brazil
Burkina Faso
Burundi
Cameroon
Cent. African Rep.
Chad
Colombia
Congo
Ecuador
Eritrea
Ethiopia
French Guiana
Gabon
Gambia
Ghana
Guinea Eq.
Guinea Bissau
Guinea Rep.
Guyana
Ivory Coast
Kenya
Liberia
Mali
Mauritania
Niger
Nigeria
Panama
Peru
Rwanda
Sao Tome & Principe
Senegal
Sierra Leone
Somalia
Sudan
Surinam
Tanzania
Togo
Uganda
Venezuela
Zaire
Zambia

Data correct as of March 1996. Always ask for current information before your trip.

COUNTRIES REPORTING

CHOLERA

many travellers think that they are likely to contract cholera while on their journey abroad. In fact, this is highly unlikely as the majority of international travellers are careful with what they eat and drink, thus reducing the risk. In general, travellers would need to ingest grossly infected water or food before they could develop the disease. Usually cholera-infected water is distinctly off-colour. Our gastric acid protects against the organism and a large quantity would usually have to be taken before infection occurs. There is a slightly higher risk in those taking acid-reducing preparations or those with a history of gastric surgery.

Officially, no country in the world requires evidence of cholera vaccination from travellers before entry. But, unofficially, many of the central African countries will look for a stamped vaccination card. Also there are reports of a similar nature from those travelling through some South American countries and also between India and Nepal by land.

Remember that it is quite possible to get cholera from eating undercooked shellfish grown in contaminated waters.

The following countries have reported cholera.

Afghanistan
Albania
Algeria
Angola
Argentina

Bangladesh

Belize

Benin Rep.

Bhutan

Bolivia

Brazil

Burkina Faso

Burma (Myanmar)

Burundi

Cambodia

Cameroon

Cape Verde

Chad

Chile

China

Colombia

Costa Rica

Djibouti

Ecuador

El Salvador

French Guiana

Gambia

Ghana

Guatemala

Guinea Bissau

Guinea Rep.

Guyana

Honduras Rep.

Hong Kong

India

Indonesia

Iran

Iraq

Ivory Coast

Kenya

Laos

Lebanon

Liberia

Malawi

Malaysia

Mali

Mauritania

Mexico

Morocco

Mozambique

Nepal

Nicaragua

Niger

Nigeria

Pakistan

Panama

Peru

Rwanda

Sao Tome & Principe

Surinam

Swaziland

Tanzania

Thailand

Togo

Tuvalu

Uganda

Ukraine

United States

Venezuela

Vietnam

Zaire

Zambia

Zimbabwe

Data correct as of March 1996. Always check for current information before your journey.

Golden rules to protect the traveller against cholera

- Clean water
- Clean food
- Clean utensils
- Clean habits

TIME ZONES

t is essential to know how many time zones you will travel across during your journey, particularly if you have some stop-overs during the flight. Adjusting your watch properly is vital if you don't want to miss your connections. Also, if you are flying for many hours you may well lose a fair amount of sleep as you cross the world's time zones.

Some of the more frequently-travelled destinations are given to be used as a guide. Remember to ask if there are any variations due to 'daylight saving time'.

Hours variation from Greenwich Mean Time

Adelaide	+9.30
Anchorage	-9
Athens	+2
Bangkok	+7
Berlin	+1
Beijing	+8
Bogota	-5
Bombay	+5.30

Buenos Aires	3		Marrakech	GMT
Cairo	+2		Mexico City	6
Calcutta	+6.30		Moscow	+3
Cape Town	+2		Nairobi	+3
Casablanca	GMT		New York	-5
Dakar	GMT		Paris	+1
Dublin	GMT		Perth	+8
Durban	+2		Quito	-5
Gibraltar	+1		Rome	+1
Harare	+2		Rio de Janeiro	-3
Hong Kong	+8		Riyadh	+3
Istanbul	+2		Santiago	-5
Jakarta	+7		Seoul	+9
Johannesburg	+2		Singapore	+7
Kinshasa	+1		Stockholm	+1
Lagos	+1		Sydney	+10
Lima	-5		Tel Aviv	+3
Lisbon	GMT		Tokyo	+9
Lusaka	+2		Tunis	+1
Manila	+8		Toronto	-5
Madrid	+1		Wellington	+12

travel
in
health

—

Section 2

While You Are Away

WHILE YOU ARE AWAY

*D*uring the time you are overseas you may be exposed to many possible dangers. Whether or not you succumb to illness depends, to a large extent, on you; what you eat, what you drink, if you are bitten by insects, where you swim and how much you sunbathe.

Over the next few chapters we will try and steer you towards the concept of healthy travelling. Enjoy yourself, experiment, but nevertheless take care.

PROBLEMS WITH AIR TRAVEL

*W*hen you travel over long distances, the alteration in time zones can be a little traumatic. Arriving at your destination at eight in the morning local time — when your body clock tells you it is midnight — means that your body and mind are conditioned for sleep. Unfortunately, your watch now tells you to get up. Add the effects of the long flight, airline food and alcohol and you may have a very tired and confused traveller. Holidays allow you to relax, but if you are there for business then you must take precautions to ensure that your mind is clear.

It is definitely best to avoid taking excessive alcohol on long-haul flights. Apart from the dehydrating effect, it also reduces your ability to walk around and exercise, a definite must if you wish to avoid possible blood clots due to staying in a sitting position for a prolonged time. Your body clock will also tell you it is time to rest while the flight staff are arriving with dinner. So what should a sensible traveller do?

Leave your watch at its original time and try to behave as you normally would relative to your watch time. This means that if your watch says 2 am, then go to sleep, irrespective of what is going on within the aircraft. This is especially important for diabetic travellers to allow them to adjust their medications. However, never forget to check the local time frequently, as otherwise you may miss some vital travel connections!

Avoid excessive eating and drinking too much alcohol. Watch the smoking too.

Exercise at regular intervals.

The swollen ankles and feet of so many travellers are mainly due to the thin air within the cabin, and the lack of exercise. Twiddle your toes and exercise the muscles right up through your body. Exercising is not always easy in a plane, but make do with what is available. Muscles can be flexed even in a sitting position by stretching your arms and physically lifting yourself up and down from your seat, using the arm rests. It may look a bit strange to your travelling companions, but you will arrive a fitter traveller.

Take plenty of decarbonated fluids. The air conditioning in the plane, and the fact that the cabin is pressurised at approximately 7,000 feet will cause you to become dehydrated. You will need the extra fluids if you want to avoid that typical, dull, muzzy head which is so common during long-haul flights.

Take enough rest when you reach your destination. If you have travelled across many time zones, your body will take time to adjust. In fact, one of the commonly accepted figures is that for each time zone you cross, your body will need one day to adjust fully. Thus a flight from London to Bangkok (seven time zones ahead of GMT) could take you up to seven days to acclimatise fully. Most healthy individuals will adapt more quickly, but certainly the first day or two will require some common sense. Don't arrange any major sightseeing for the first 24 hours, and, if it is a business trip, don't plan to make any major decisions within the first day or so after you arrive.

When you travel from west to east your watch will need to go forward. Flying east to west your watch will need to go back a number of hours. In both cases you run the risk of disturbing your natural bio-rhythms and ending up having a very long day after you arrive. Again stick to your biological time clock if possible and take a day or two to adjust to your new environment.

Current medications are not very effective in counter-acting jet lag. However, within the next few years there may be more effective tablets available. These tablets are based on the use of a natural hormone within the body — melatonin. However, until such drugs are developed, normal requirements for rest mean that long-haul jet travel will continue to pose problems for the ill prepared.

FOOD-BORNE

DISEASE

One of the great delights of foreign travel is the ability to savour local food cooked in its natural manner and surroundings. The excitement of delving into the unknown is nowhere more easily seen than when faced with a bowl of who knows what in the middle of who knows where. The warnings you received before leaving home about tasting the unknown go sailing out the window. In many cases only the next few days will really tell how sensible you have been. Forewarned, however, is forearmed.

What is the chance of the traveller becoming ill with a significant diarrhoeal disease? The World Health Organisation would put the figure close to 30%. This does not mean that a third of travellers will become moribund but, nevertheless, a large number will have their holiday plans disturbed significantly due to a dose of diarrhoea. How can you go about steering clear of potential food-borne dangers but at the same time not lessen the enjoyment of your journey?

In regard to foods overseas your motto should be experiment, but with great care. So long as you are sensible, your holiday can be both safe and satisfying. It is very common to hear travellers say that they will be staying in five star hotels, or will only be visiting the better safari camps and so the food will be perfect. This is foolish. Without any doubt, the weakest point in the chain is in the kitchens, no matter how expensive the place is or how clean the lobby staff may appear. How many travellers have the opportunity to wander around the kitchens unannounced?

The weakness may be either from the hygiene of the staff or old and inefficient cooking and storage systems; but there are other questions to be considered. How many kitchen staff are there for the size of the hotel? What is the state of the hygiene facilities for the kitchen staff? How efficient are the refrigerators and the cookers? How often are the kitchen and serving staff medically screened?

These are questions which most travellers will not ask. So the golden rule is: ALL food should be cooked recently and thoroughly and screened from contact with flies and unnecessary food handlers. Drinks should be light alcohol, sealed mineral waters, sodas or, of course, hot beverages like tea or coffee.

With apartment holidays you personally are responsible for food purchase and preparation. The food-borne risks tend to revolve around the times you eat out. Remember that in a hot climate food will go off more quickly. What might have been a safe practice at home may not be at all safe in regions where the temperatures are constantly in the high 20s.

If you have chosen to stay in a hotel rather than self-catering, no matter how great the place looks in the brochure, how can you tell what the place is really like? The most important thing is to try and understand the risks of developing a food-borne disease and how to steer a path away from the more obvious troublemakers.

Hot food

As a good basic rule, food which is hot and fresh will be safe. The correct temperatures must have been reached and it must not have been allowed to cool in an area where contamination might have occurred. Cold meats are a high risk as they provide the ideal environment for the cultivation of many bacteria. The hot, steaming, meat dish will usually be fine unless the meat is really off, and that should be fairly obvious even before the first bite. Never feel you must finish the meal just because you have paid for it — you may end up paying twice!

Thin slices of meat are safer as the cooking will have more of a chance to penetrate right through. Never ask for undercooked, or rare meat, as the risk of tape worm infestation is just too high. Certainly any portion of the meat which comes still bloody should either be left at the side of your plate (and put down to experience), or returned for re-cooking. Just make sure you get your own meal back.

Cold food

In many areas your meat dish will be served with a side order of salad. The best advice is to push the salad to one side and leave it alone. It will look really tempting but the risks are too high. One particular risk relates to contamination occurring while the vegetables are being grown. Human excreta (night soil) is frequently used as a fertiliser and many of the more potent bugs (protozoa) will be easily transmitted in this way. The cysts of these bugs (especially amoeba and giardia) appear to soak into the lettuce leaf and simple washing in clean water may not be enough to kill them off. It is safer to soak the lettuce in a weak solution of chlorine and then wash the leaf in clean water. How many hotels do you think go to this much trouble?

One other risk revolves around the handling of cold foods including lettuce, tomatoes, onions, peppers, etc. Contamination may occur from contact with food handlers who may not have washed their hands properly. A golden rule for travellers: steer clear of salads.

Shellfish

Sampling shellfish abroad is high on the pleasure list of many travellers. Is it safe? How high is the risk? Are there no exceptions? Again, the short answer is to avoid all undercooked shellfish like the plague. They are a regular source of trouble for the traveller but the risks can easily be understood. Most shellfish rely on their filtration system to harvest their own food from the water in which they live. In general the bivalve shellfish (mussels, prawns, oysters, etc.) live close to the shoreline. In many areas throughout the world the sewage drainage system may not be piped out far enough from the shoreline, or alternatively there may be strong currents heading back towards the coast. Whatever the cause, it is common for the contaminated water to come into contact with the local shellfish. The shellfish filter the water to gain nutrients for their own survival and in doing so may become contaminated with human sewage. If these shellfish are harvested for human consumption they may be transported many miles from the point of original contamination. For many dishes, the shellfish is steamed rather than fully heated and deep sterilisation frequently will not occur. Under these circumstances the

traveller will end up eating what amounts to raw human sewage! The major infectious diseases which are spread in this way include typhoid, cholera and hepatitis A. Meals of lobster and crab do not tend to suffer as the dish is usually well boiled. Fried prawns may also be safe, depending on the extent of the cooking. Stir fry meals are notorious for under-cooking, so again, beware.

Fish meals tend to be fairly safe as the meat is soft and easily cooked right through. Just remember, though, that sushi (raw fish) is a delicacy in parts of the Far East. Some may contain parasites which are very rare. This means that these conditions are very difficult to diagnose, let alone treat, back at home. Be adventurous, but always make sure your meal is well cooked.

the display, the greater the risk due to handling by the kitchen staff. If you really want to indulge yourself then burrow down to the lower levels of the display and choose the fruit which will have been protected from potential contamination by previous guests and staff alike.

Flies are frequently associated with food contamination. If you see many flies in the hotel, and especially in the eating areas, then be very suspicious of the level of hygiene. Also check the knives, forks and spoons; especially the forks which are the hardest to clean. The cleanliness of chop sticks is particularly difficult to judge. Again be extremely cautious.

In any part of the world if you want to check out the level of hygiene of an establishment, the best place to start is the guest toi-

Fruit

Many of the hotter areas of our world have an abundance of fruit, also one of the great joys of international travel. Is there a risk? Of course. Can you minimise the risk? Definitely.

So long as your hands are clean, then any fruit with intact skin which you peel yourself should be safe. The danger lies in eating fruit which others have kindly peeled for you and prepared in gorgeous displays. Remember the more splendid

lets. If they are below standard then can you imagine the state of the staff facilities? If you have to stay and eat then at least make sure that you have a small supply of moist, foil-wrapped tissues and wash your hands and even the cutlery if necessary.

Dairy produce

When it is hot, ice cream is one of the greatest temptations, even though you know that ice cream and dairy produce may be harmful. If you decide that taking the risk is better than dying of thirst then at least follow your common sense and choose to buy from established shops or restaurants. Choose well-wrapped items and a well known name if possible. Never eat ice cream cones.

Even dairy products such as cheese, butter, milk and yoghurt can all spell disaster while abroad. Again if you choose the better brands, and eat only well-sealed butter and cheese, the risks will usually be less. Yoghurt is often used to settle an upset stomach, and due to its higher acid content, it is thought to be relatively safer than some other dairy products. Milk needs to be pasteurised to be safe. Unpasteurised milk may spread serious diseases such as tuberculosis and brucellosis. The UHT milk is almost always safe so long as the container is intact. It will also last for many weeks if unopened and is therefore ideal for travelling.

Street vendors

Pictures of street vendors feature prominently in any book or lecture on the risks facing the international traveller, and for very good reasons. They are probably one of the most common sources of contamination and you would do well to steer clear.

Hygiene is very limited when it comes to buying food or drink in the street. The food storage is poor and contamination frequently occurs while the trolley is being packed and from the dirty hands selling the items. How sterile are the glasses? How are they cleaned if they are not disposable?

This does not mean you have to starve while abroad. There are many foods which you can eat and many new tastes to try. Any food which can be peeled; from boiled eggs to oranges, avocado to pineapple, will be safe.

Golden rules:
- Eat what you recognise
- Stick to hot foods (physically hot, not spicy!)
- Avoid all salads
- Never eat undercooked meat dishes
- Well-cooked fish is usually safer than meat
- Take extra care with stir-fry meals
- Avoid undercooked shellfish dishes, especially prawns, mussels, shrimps and oysters
- Only eat fruit you peel yourself
- Never eat food from street vendors
- Always choose thin slices of meat
- Eat only in clean restaurants
- Wash your hands before you eat
- Check the cutlery before you order your meal
- If possible, ask your representative's advice about local foods

W

DISEASE

*W*ater is probably the traveller's single worst enemy. If you treat it with the greatest of respect then there is a good chance that you will get on well together.

Remember that very often the water supply may not be contaminated but it is the variation in fluoride and calcium which will cause problems for travellers. This can occur even on the shortest holiday away from home, and not just on the tropical or inter-continental holiday. It all depends on the sensitivity of your stomach. If you are one of those unfortunates with a weak stomach then take extra care.

How can you tell safe fluids from those which should be avoided? Is it safe to drink the hotel tap water? What about the jug of 'filtered' water which is brought fresh to your room each morning? Are mineral waters safe? How much fluid should you be drinking anyhow?

On most inter-continental or

tropical holidays, travellers tend to become dehydrated and it is at these times — when the defences are down — that almost any fluid which looks inviting may be consumed.

How much fluid do you need each day?

This depends on many factors including the ambient temperature, the humidity factor and your own degree of exertion. In general terms, in a temperate climate an adult will require 2 - 3 litres of fluid each day for normal metabolism. This fluid comes in the form of water, tea, coffee, minerals, etc. as well as within the food we consume.

In a hotter climate, it is essential to maintain an adequate fluid intake, the level of which will increase due to perspiration. Up to 4 or 5 litres may be required; perhaps even more. This also depends on the type of holiday you take. Lying beside the pool all day is not the same as hiking up and down the pyramids! A large amount of salt is also lost in perspiration and you will need to increase your intake to maintain supplies. The body will keep the levels steady for as long as it can by taking salt from within the cells, but after a while you will begin to experience symptoms and signs of salt depletion. You may find that you become tired, irritable and perhaps develop some muscle cramps, usually in the second week. Most travellers just put this down to doing too much and so they restrict their activities. Such reactions are simply the body's own built-in safety mechanism.

Assuming that you have no serious heart trouble or a history of hypertension then it may be worthwhile increasing the amount of salt you take on your food. Don't use salt tablets except under expert medical supervision as it is very easy to overdose.

The hotel tap water

It would be untrue to say that all hotel tap water overseas is unsafe. In many of the major tourist areas of the world the better hotels have a water supply which would rival ours at home. In these cases the risk from using the water will be very small. So how can you tell if it is safe?

Firstly, always check with the local representative for your tour company. They don't want you to fall ill so they tend to be very cautious. However, don't forget that variations in the water supply do frequently occur and what was safe yesterday may not be safe today.

The easiest precaution is to smell the cold water supply in your room. If you can smell chlorine then it should be safe. At times you may actually smell sewage; it would be unwise to use this water for anything more than the most basic of tasks, and that does not include brushing your teeth!

The hotel water jug

This is another cause for concern. The best advice is still to exercise caution and avoid using the water for drinking or brushing your teeth. In most hotels with 100 or more bedrooms, it would be too time consuming for the staff to boil and filter water for each room, so standard tap water is frequently used.

In some of the better hotels a sand filtration system may be in use but, in general, the extent of the filtration is so poor that many viruses, protozoa and bacteria can escape into the 'pure' water. It is not worth the risk.

Mineral waters

Most travellers nowadays will look for mineral water and use this as their main source of water for their holiday. This is usually a very safe option. Just make sure, however, that the bottle has not been opened, used and then refilled with tap water. Check the seal is intact and could not have been tampered with prior to purchase. This also applies to soft drinks sold outdoors. Using the sparkling mineral waters or sodas solves this problem as when they are opened you should hear that encouraging 'hiss'.

Minerals

If you can find cans with any of the better known mineral names, you will be able to quench your thirst, confident in the knowledge that the fluids will be pure and that the risk of contamination is minimal. Don't forget though, that the outside of the can may have been cooled in ice made from grossly contaminated water so try and use straws or at least clean the can lip as much as possible before you indulge.

With bottles it is not quite such a safe bet. If the name on the lid does not match the name on the bottle, then beware. It is important to recognise that if the bottle and lid names are the same then the risk is very small, as the major mineral groups are scrupulously careful in ensuring that their drinks are of the highest standard.

One final word of caution with regard to bottles. If you order minerals, watch how the bottles are carried to your table. In many areas it is a custom to put fingers into the neck of bottles to carry them to your table. This is not a very wise practice unless you know that the fingers have just been through a steriliser!

Is ice safe?

This depends on the water supply of the area. It is more sensible to assume that the water is unsafe, in which case so will the ice made from it, as freezing does not sufficiently sterilise water. While abroad always ask for drinks without ice. If the drink is brought to your table with ice, accept it without too much fuss. If you refuse the drinks, potentially what will happen is that the waiter will retreat around the corner, dunk his fingers into your drink, remove the ice cubes and then return with your 'fresh' drink. Now you have the potential contamination from the ice and also the much higher risk from those fingers. Just smile sweetly, accept the drink and remove the ice yourself into the ashtray. The amount of contamination from that small exposure will be negligible.

If you want to make ice yourself then use either boiled water or mineral water. These should be quite safe.

Water fountains

Travellers who use communal water fountains will almost certainly need both their head and their bowels examined. The risk from previous mouths is just too high no matter how much you try and clean them.

Fruit drinks

In the better hotels, the freshly-squeezed fruit drinks are a great thirst-quencher. However, if you are off the beaten track and offered a fruit drink, take care; the fruit juice may have been supplemented with tap water and perhaps some sugar. This addition of the local water may be disastrous.

Brushing your teeth

Many travellers are meticulous in watching their fluid intake and ensuring that sterility is top of their list at all times. However, they often lapse by using the unsafe tap water for brushing their teeth. 'I'm not going to swallow it' is the usual comment. What is not under-

stood is that any water contact within the mouth is available for absorption at a very rapid rate and significant contamination can occur very easily. If you believe that the water is unsafe for drinking then don't use it for brushing your teeth either.

If you feel that you just have to use tap water for brushing your teeth, then it is probably safer to use the hot water tap as at least the water may have been slightly sterilised and therefore a little safer.

We all need water constantly. Don't forget that the vast majority of your body mass is made up from water and dehydration can occur very easily in the unwary. Just watch the amount of your intake and ensure that the fluids you consume are safe and all should be well.

Golden rules

- Assume all tap water may be contaminated
- Smell the tap water for a clean chlorine smell
- If suspicious, don't drink the tap water or use it to brush your teeth
- Check that mineral water is sealed when purchased
- Use branded mineral drinks
- Local beers are usually safe
- Avoid the hotel water jug
- Never open your mouth in the shower
- Use straws wherever possible
- Clean the bottle neck before you drink
- Minerals in cans are always safe unless previously opened
- Drink only pasteurised dairy products

INSECT-BORNE DISEASE

*O*ne of the main reasons why many people may not take an international holiday is their fear of insects. It may not be just the bite, but also the severe reaction which can subsequently occur. There is no reason to avoid hot countries as many biting insects also abound in many of the colder climates — you may be troubled no matter where you go.

Mosquitoes are the main problem, but there is a plethora of other bloodsuckers which can also irritate. Many of them are actually downright dangerous.

The list includes sandflys, tsetse flies, ticks, fleas, bed-bugs, ants and some of the larger cockroach-type insects.

It is worth remembering that there is only one reason why insects take blood — they need the nutrients for either their own development or for their offspring. Nevertheless, they really are a nuisance and taking care to protect yourself against them is well worth the trouble. Also remember that not all bites will cause infection. In many cases the only problem is the allergic reaction to the insect's saliva which is injected under the skin. This is used to thin the blood and make it easier to suck out.

Although most of the blood-sucking insects bite at either dusk or dawn, they can bite at any time. Travellers in parts of Africa may be unsure as to what particular insect has bitten them; was it a mosquito or perhaps a tsetse fly? The difference is clear. Generally a mosquito lands and will usually bite very quickly and just about painlessly. On the other hand, a tsetse fly lands, seems to smell you for a while and then sticks a power drill into you.

Mosquitoes

There is no doubt that mosquitoes are the biggest single worry for most travellers. Their size and ability to squeeze through the smallest hole makes them a menace. Many a traveller has been forced into hospital because of a severe reaction to the bite of this lowly insect.

There are hundreds of different types of mosquito and they are involved in transmitting a whole series of diseases to man. Malaria is the best known but others include yellow fever, filariasis, dengue fever, St. Louis encephalitis and Japanese B encephalitis, to name just a few. The male of the species does not bite. The female, on the other hand, is a ferocious feeder. Telling the difference between the male and female is not an easy task for the inexperienced, so squashing both is probably the best course of action.

In most of the major capital cities of the tropics there are few mosquitoes. The risk may be lower if you stay in the city but many travellers tend to wander, thus increasing the danger. Watch out in the market places particularly. Golf courses are also excellent breeding sites for mosquitoes and many ardent golfers tend to play close to either dusk or dawn, the cooler hours when mosquitoes usually bite. Unfortunately, some other species prefer to bite during the heat of the day.

Sandflies

These little, hairy insects are about one third the size of a mosquito and can penetrate through the normal mosquito net. There are special small-mesh sandfly nets but they restrict air flow and can be quite claustrophobic. The sandfly tends to hover around your ankle and enjoys a good blood meal. You will hardly feel this little creature when it lands and feeds. Sandflies are most common in rural areas, especially where there are sand and clay banks which make perfect homes for rodents, usually the

sandfly's preferred host.

Sandflies don't like the direct sun too much and so they are not a particular problem during the heat of daytime, although they can hover close to swimming pools in the shaded areas. On cloudy days, however, they emerge. One of the main diseases transmitted by the sandfly is leishmaniasis and this can affect the skin or deeper organs. Transmission occurs in most of the hotter areas of the world and it should be remembered that this includes most of the Mediterranean coastline. Symptoms of leishmaniasis include either slow-healing skin ulcers or enlargement of some of the deeper organs. Symptoms and signs may not occur for many months after the bites.

Tsetse flies

These are a bit like an overgrown housefly which bites. The

tsetse lives across tropical Africa and also needs blood for its offspring. They bite humans and animals, and it is the tsetse fly which transmits sleeping sickness (trypanosomiasis) to both. This can be a very serious illness and the main early sign is an abscess or sore in the region of a bite from a large fly.

In general the tsetse fly will be attracted towards darker clothing and also a moving object. One of the most common danger times is standing in the back of a moving vehicle while viewing animals on safari in East Africa. Still, despite this, it is true to say that very few cases of an infected tsetse fly bite are seen in travellers returning from safari holidays in Africa. Just remember that there is a risk, so take care.

Ticks

Most holidaymakers will not be bitten by ticks while overseas. Those mainly at risk are the trekkers wandering through the outback regions. Ticks occur almost everywhere throughout the world and they are involved in the transmission of many exotic diseases. They really are the dirtiest creatures and you should do your best to avoid them.

Usually transmission occurs when travellers are walking through bracken-covered countryside or from close contact with animals. The tick grabs onto an exposed skin surface and will commence drinking once firmly attached. It appears that many ticks need time to settle themselves before they start to feed and early removal of the tick lessens the risk of potential infection. The actual time factor varies but in many cases it may be up to 24 hours. Don't sit watching the bug, get rid of it as soon as possible.

Never grasp any tick by its

body and pull. You may just inject the body contents of the tick into the recipient and probably also yank the head off the insect's body which will lead to more problems. Try to wait until you have a small tweezers and grasp the tick by its head parts and hopefully it should come free in one piece. Clean the area and then apply an antiseptic or antibiotic cream. If you are in an area where ticks transmit infection, consult a doctor and see if further therapy may be required. Vaseline has also been used to stop the tick breathing and it will then usually fall off fairly easily.

Fleas and bed-bugs

If you have bites in regions of your body which are usually kept covered, such as your back or buttocks, consider the possibility of insects other than mosquitoes. Fleas and bed-bugs are the most common. Fleas are nearly always

associated with animals, so see if there is a dog or cat sneaking into your room and snuggling down on your bed during the day. If you believe the mattress is infested with bed-bugs, try and place it out in direct sunlight, as they are easily killed off by bright light. Even a fairly bright cloudy day should give them a good scare.

Ants, lizards and cockroaches

Again, travellers seldom have problems from these creatures as lizards and cockroaches will rarely approach humans. In fact,

they can be very useful, especially lizards which eat small insects like mosquitoes, so don't kill them.

You will only come across ants if you are out walking and happen to stray off the beaten track. If so, you are delving into their territory and are liable to be bitten. Ant bites are more of a nuisance than downright dangerous, unless you have fallen over drunk directly in the path of army ants, that is. Cockroaches may spread infection as they wander around between animal faeces and your food.

Protection against insect bites

The rules for avoiding insects are very similar, regardless of type. Cover your skin where possible; insects don't usually tend to bite through clothing as it blunts their proboscis.

Cover the exposed areas with an insect repellent when necessary. The insect repellent usually recommended contains a substance known as diethyl-toluamide or DEET. It has been shown that a concentration of over 30% is usually required to stop the insects landing. DEET should not be used near the eyes and, if over-used, high concentrations may be absorbed through the skin which may cause problems. You should not need insect repellent while sleeping at night time, so wash it off before you retire. If there are mosquitoes in your room, deal with them and seal the room from further attackers.

If there is a mosquito net over your bed, use it. Make sure there are no holes and that you tuck the net under your mattress. (By the way, don't tuck the net in too well if you have a touch of the Delhi belly. There is nothing worse than struggling to free the well-secured net in the middle of the night as you try to dash for the loo!)

When you reach your destination, buy a small can of insect repellent and squirt the centre of the room, door frame and curtains before you leave for your evening meal. Keep the window closed and turn off the air conditioner until you return. At this stage the room should be free of insects and you can turn the air conditioner back on before enjoying a quiet night's sleep. It is also wise to tuck your net under the mattress at this early stage in the evening before the mosquitoes really come out.

The electric insect repellents which work by heating a coil are very effective and are a simple way of protecting the room. Just make sure you have the correct voltage for your destination.

If there is an air conditioner in your room, make sure that it is set at a cold enough level. Some hotels will set the machine at a warmer temperature to save money but this will not provide sufficient protection.

Electronic buzzers appear to have no effect in repelling mosquitoes.

Always carry a small torch in case of a power failure.

What to do if bitten

As we mentioned earlier, the main initial effect following an insect bite is related to the traveller's allergy to the saliva which has been injected under the skin. If you can treat the bite area as soon as possible you will usually lessen the severity of the response.

- Clean the area
- Apply a steroid/antibiotic or antihistamine cream immediately
- If necessary, take antihistamine tablets

- Most of the time this will be sufficient, but for some travellers there may be a case for commencing antihistamines before their exposure. Talk this through with your doctor during your initial consultation.

Summary

Basically, insects are our friends! At times it may not feel this way but they help to keep the status quo in our environment and their wholesale destruction would not be to our benefit. Obviously, however, we should be careful to try and lessen the opportunities for their feeding on us. Taking good care and treating any bites early will help to reduce the severity of your symptoms and allow you to enjoy your holiday.

Golden rules

- Where possible, avoid going outside between dusk and dawn
- Wear long-sleeved clothing
- Avoid dark colours, which tend to attract insects
- If possible choose an air-conditioned room
- Use insect repellents, but not in excess
- If there are mosquito nets, use them
- Permethrin-dipped nets are more effective
- Securely close any screens on the windows and doors before dusk
- Use anti-mosquito sprays on the windows, doors and curtains
- Use electric insect repellents. Buzzers are not recommended
- Above the third floor, flying insects are not usually a problem
- Treat insect bites at an early stage
- Carry antihistamines if you are usually badly affected

THE RISK OF MALARIA

*m*alaria is usually transmitted by the bite of the infected female anophiline mosquito. The disease is rampant in many of the warmer areas of the world and travellers will frequently be exposed to it during their journey. The risk of malaria should not cause travellers to cancel their journey, but it is common sense to understand the basics of the disease and to realise the ways that it can be contracted.

Life cycle

The disease is caused by a small single-celled organism which invades our body. The organism is usually transmitted through the bite of a mosquito but transmission can also occur through a transfusion of infected blood.

The organism is injected into the human within the mosquito's saliva and it then travels very rapidly to the liver where it penetrates the cells and multiplies dramatically. This multiplication in the liver may take days or weeks depending on the type of malaria involved. After this part of the life cycle, the parasite bursts out of the liver cell and penetrates the

73

red blood cells where it multiplies. Finally it ruptures the cell, only to go on to invade more red blood cells. The major symptoms associated with malaria (fever, chills, sweats, etc.) are linked with the destruction of the red blood cells and the release of toxic compounds into the bloodstream.

Eventually the parasite will either kill off too many red blood cells for the human to survive, or else the body's defences will take over. Problems will only occur when the parasite starts to break down the red blood cells. This may be up to many weeks or months after infection occurred.

Clinical symptoms

The only symptom the traveller may initially experience is irritation at the mosquito bite. However, this allergic reaction may occur after any insect bite and not just a mosquito's. Also, it

is worth remembering that many travellers will not show any reaction to insect bites and they may, mistakenly, feel they have not been bitten. This can be a fatal error. The initial signs of malaria can also be confused with the effects of excessive alcohol consumption.

Signs and symptoms

Typically the patient will develop signs of a severe dose of influenza, such as headache, muscular aches and pains, hot and cold attacks and bouts of severe sweating. There are also a multitude of other signs and symptoms which include mild jaundice, nausea, vomiting, diarrhoea and generalised weakness.

In fact, patients may present with all manner of symptoms, but the one cardinal sign is fever. In only very exceptional cases will fever be absent.

Making a diagnosis

The only definite way to make a diagnosis is to examine the blood under a microscope to find the parasite. In some areas it is very difficult to trust the local laboratories and so a definite diagnosis may not be possible.

Any patient who falls ill with a fever either in the tropics or following their return, should be suspected of having contracted malaria until it is proved otherwise. Blood should be taken and expertly assessed for the presence of malaria parasites. It may be necessary to commence adequate chemotherapy even before the diagnosis is proved. At times the parasites may not show in the blood sample. Careful medical attention is required to decide on the most suitable treatment. Giving chemotherapy to patients who just have influenza will not usually cause major harm but withholding suitable therapy from patients with malaria may have disastrous consequences.

Travellers who plan longer trips overseas, or those on trekking holidays may be given a standby treatment to carry with them. This treatment dose is usually only required in exceptional circumstances when the traveller becomes very ill and no adequate medical attention is available. Always take the possibility of malaria seriously.

Protecting the traveller

Most of this section is covered in the chapter 'Insect-borne Disease' but malaria tablets are important for many journeys. The tablets need to be taken for a few days before the traveller is exposed, continued regularly while abroad and maintained for at least four weeks after the traveller leaves the malarial zone.

This is because of the parasite's life cycle in the liver and the possibility that the parasite may only reach the bloodstream many weeks after infection. There are many different types of tablets used for malaria prophylaxis.

Malaria prophylaxis

The main way to protect yourself against malaria is to avoid being bitten. Nevertheless your doctor may prescribe tablets to help protect you against the disease. If this is the case, make certain you take them regularly. The most common four drugs which are currently used (1996) are described briefly in the following paragraphs.

Chloroquine

This drug has been in widespread use for many years. Unfortunately, its effectiveness has recently decreased due to widespread resistance by the malaria parasite. Nevertheless, it is still the major drug for parts of northern Africa, some regions in the Middle East and areas north of the Panama Canal. It is taken once a week, usually starting the Sunday before exposure commences, then each Sunday throughout the risk time and finally for a full four weeks after leaving the malarial zone. There are very few side-effects but some patients complain of headaches, irritated skin and, occasionally, hair loss. Current advice suggests that chloroquine should not be used for more than six years due to its reported ability to cause eye problems. The most significant side-effect is the fact that chloroquine tastes obnoxious.

Proguanil

This is probably the safest but weakest of the drugs used for malaria prophylaxis. The drug needs to be taken each day and, again, it has a very distinct taste. Proguanil and chloroquine appear to be the safest drugs to be used during all stages of pregnancy. The drug is commenced a few days before exposure, continued each day while in the malaria transmission zone and then, also, for a full four weeks after leaving.

Mefloquine

This is one of the newest drugs on the market to protect against malaria. The drug is given as one tablet each week. There are some contraindications with the use of mefloquine. Those who are pregnant, wish to become pregnant within three months or who are breast feeding should not use mefloquine until further safety information is available. It is also contraindicated in those with a history of epilepsy or certain other serious neurological illnesses. Patients with a history of serious mood-swing disorders should also not take mefloquine. This list sounds as though mefloquine should never be used, but this is not the case. It has been in widespread use for several years and as long as travellers are selected carefully, it appears that the risk of side-effects is minimal. Like chloroquine, mefloquine is usually taken a few weeks before exposure, once each week while away and for a further four weeks after leaving the malarial zone. It is probably wise to restrict alcohol intake for 24 hours before and after taking the weekly mefloquine to lessen the risk of any reaction.

Doxycycline

This is one of the more potent tetracycline antibiotics which has been shown to be very useful in providing protection against malaria. It needs to be used daily and there are few significant side-effects. Some patients develop diarrhoea and thrush but this is not usual. Doxycycline is started a few days before exposure, continued throughout the time in the risk area and then, again, for a full four weeks after leaving the region.

However, protection against mosquito bites is essential as no tablets provide full protection against malaria. Even with that in mind, the disease can still occur although the traveller has done everything possible to protect him- or herself. Any unusual symptoms which occur for at least a year after a foreign trip may be due to infection contracted abroad and should be investigated with this in mind. Always tell your doctor about any foreign travel during the recent past.

Golden rules

If you are prescribed tablets:

- Don't miss doses of malaria pills
- Start at least a week before you travel, take them regularly while you are at risk and continue them for a further four weeks after you leave the area (these final four weeks are essential)
- Try to avoid all mosquito bites

If you have been badly bitten, tell your doctor on your return home.

- Look out for symptoms such as fever, sweating attacks, headaches, joint aches and pains and shivering
- An attack may only start weeks or months after you return home Even though you have obeyed all the rules, this still does not give full protection
- Malaria can kill — take care

MALARIA

INFECTED COUNTRIES

R denotes countries with resistant malaria. More countries are likely to report resistance, so request current information before your journey.

Afghanistan	R
Algeria	
Angola	R
Argentina	
Bangladesh	R
Belize	
Benin Rep.	R
Bhutan	R
Bolivia	R
Botswana	R
Brazil	R
Burkina Faso	R
Burma (Myanmar)	R
Burundi	R
Cambodia	R
Cameroon	R
Cent. African Rep.	R
Chad	R
China	R
Colombia	R
Comoros	R
Congo	R
Costa Rica	
Djibouti	R
Dominican Rep.	
Ecuador	R
Egypt	
El Salvador	
Ethiopia	R
Eritrea	R
French Guiana	R
Gabon	R
Gambia	R
Ghana	R
Guatemala	
Guinea Eq.	R
Guinea Bissau	R
Guyana	R
Haiti	
Honduras Rep.	
India	R
Indonesia	R

MALARIA INFECTED COUNTRIES

Iran	R	Rwanda	R
Iraq		Sao Tome & Principe	R
Ivory Coast	R	Saudi Arabia	R
Kenya	R	Senegal	R
Laos	R	Sierra Leone	R
Liberia	R	Solomon Is.	R
Libya		Somalia	R
Madagascar	R	South Africa	R
Malawi	R	Sri Lanka	R
Malaysia	R	Sudan	R
Mali	R	Surinam	R
Mauritania	R	Swaziland	R
Mauritius		Syria	
Mayotte	R	Tanzania	R
Mexico		Thailand	R
Morocco		Togo	R
Mozambique	R	Turkey	
Namibia	R	Uganda	R
Nepal	R	United Arab Em.	
Nicaragua		Vanuatu	R
Niger	R	Venezuela	R
Nigeria	R	Vietnam	R
Oman	R	Yemen	R
Pakistan	R	Zaire	R
Panama	R	Zambia	R
Papua New Guinea	R	Zimbabwe	R
Paraguay			
Peru	R		
Philippines	R		
Russia			

Data correct as of March 1996. Always check for current details before your journey.

S ON HOLIDAY

One of the hallmarks of a good holiday for many people is swimming. Nevertheless there are risks and naturally care must be taken to ensure that silly and potentially dangerous mistakes are limited, if not fully avoided.

The risks are related to where you swim and the safety factors of the area.

Swimming pools

It is probably true to say that these are the safest places to bathe. Swimming pools in many regions are clean, safe and have good life-guard cover. The risk of drowning or infection is very small but certain basic care is needed.

Are there life guards on duty whenever the pool is open for swimming? How well is the pool maintained? Are the water filters clogged? Is the pool well chlorinated? Can you see the bottom at the deep end? Is there any tree cover close to the pool to protect bathers from the sun? Are diving and jumping allowed? Is the perimeter of the pool excessively slippery? What are the changing facilities and lavatories like? Is the poolside catering hygiene adequate? Never let children out of your sight even for a few seconds.

Travellers often ask questions about the risk of picking up infection from swimming pools. In general this is regarded as unlikely, and certainly, if the pool is sufficiently chlorinated, transmission should not be a problem. Nevertheless, some travellers have very sensitive eyes and may develop a conjunctivitis after swimming. This could be due to chemical agents (such as chlorine) or infection. In both cases using goggles and a simple eye bathing solution after your swim will usually lessen the effects.

Never drink the pool water.

The sea

Don't underestimate the power of the sea. Local currents may not be at all obvious until it is too late. Look out for warning signs and never be the lone swimmer furthest from the shore. Swimming out to the coral reefs is a common mistake made by many travellers. The currents in these areas can change suddenly and be stronger than even the best swimmer can combat. Get good local advice.

The sea is home to many creatures whose territory you are invading, not the other way round. Jellyfish, sharks, sea urchins and sea snakes all deserve respect.

Look out for dirt on the sea shore. It may be that the local sewage drainage is inadequate and so contamination frequently occurs in the tourist swimming areas. Look out for dogs and other animals by the sea. They may soil the beach and contaminate the shoreline with their parasites. Tourists can pick up some of these parasites through their skin and develop a nasty skin rash. It is wise to wear flip-flops or something similar on the beach area especially above the high tide mark. Lie on a towel or a sun bed rather than straight on the sand.

Scuba diving is becoming more popular but it is risky. Before you undertake a dive make certain you are well prepared. If you have never dived before, stick with the lessons for beginners. If you are going out in a boat, either wear a life jacket or don't go far from the coast.

Freshwater rivers and lakes

Most of the risks revolve around either the chance of an exotic parasitic infection, or an unexpected meeting with a hungry crocodile. The main parasitic infection which may occur from swimming in freshwater rivers and lakes is schistosomiasis, also known as bilharzia, after the German pathologist who first identified the parasite. This infection occurs mainly in Africa, parts of Asia and South America. Usually transmission is from freshwater contact in lakes or rivers with slow-moving water. Nevertheless any freshwater expanse in these regions may be capable of harbouring the parasite and swimming should not be encouraged. Asking the locals is not always helpful. In general they will say it is safe and they have being swimming there for years!

The main danger spots for transmission are close to reeds and where the water is moving slowly. This does not mean that disease transmission will not occur in the centre of a river, but perhaps it is slightly safer. The only thing is; how do you get to the centre?

The little parasite which is involved in schistosomiasis is released by certain species of snails. It is then capable of penetrating intact human skin into the body. Swimmers may notice an itch developing within 24 hours and this is one sign that they should seek medical attention. Even without this itch any traveller exposed to freshwater while in these regions should request medical attention on their return. This does not just mean swimming; exposure can also occur while pushing your car out of a flooded river or even from paddling, so be careful.

Crocodiles are certainly best

would not harm a soul. Don't be fooled. Steer clear of them in water; they have a very nasty bite! Another note of caution; don't go between a hippo and its water supply. They tend to suddenly charge back to the water regardless of anything in their way.

General notes

1. Never swim beyond your ability.

2. Never swim straight after a meal. Usually wait about two hours. What is actually happening is that as the food is passing through your stomach, blood is diverted to the intestines so that metabolism can occur. If you then exercise, the blood supply to your mus-

avoided. There are many stories each year from tropical Africa and the Far East of people being attacked while swimming in rivers and lakes. If there is any suggestion of crocodiles in the area, don't go into the water and take care close to the banks. It might also be prudent to issue a short warning about hippos. These are usually docile creatures and look as though they cles may be inadequate and so spasm easily occurs.

3. Don't dive into any water without checking the depth. Many spinal fractures are caused by swimmers diving into shallow water and breaking their necks.

4. If you have ear problems then don't dive into the pool or swim down to the depths at the deep end. Keep a set of ear plugs handy and use them each time you swim. If you use ear plugs, keep your wits about you while swimming — they may stop you hearing warnings from fellow bathers.

Golden rules

- Never swim unless you are certain it is safe

- Ask your representative's advice if possible

- Check the pool is chlorinated and clean

- Never swim in freshwater rivers or lakes in central Africa, parts of Asia and South America because of the risks of parasitic disease

- Don't walk through flooded rivers unless you have to

- If swimming in the sea, look out for jellyfish, water snakes and, of course, sharks

- Never swim after drinking alcohol

- Watch out for strong local currents

- Don't get sunburnt while swimming

- Never swim alone

SUN EXPOSURE

"For a feeling that makes you very much alive, sensitive to every movement of your being and aware of the vibrations of your environment, there is nothing like a good sunburn"

Reproduced in the Readers Digest May 1992 from an article by Paul Sweeney in The Quarterly.

i t is wise firstly to dispel the fallacy that there is any such a thing as a 'good sunburn'. A more appropriate term would be 'skin burn'. No sunburn can be beneficial for our skin. The sun can be extremely strong in the tropics and the harmful ultraviolet rays are known to be a cause of cancer.

This of course does not mean that you must remain covered from head to foot. However, like anything else in life our problems arise from over-exposure, over-

consumption or over-indulgence. We remain working away for the majority of the year, earning enough to escape and then when we do, we go mad, trying to soak in as much as possible in as short a time as possible and this includes the sun.

Who?

Anyone can become sunburnt, especially on areas of our bodies which are unaccustomed to seeing the light of day in our own climate: areas like the tops of the legs, the ankles and elbows, the neck, the nose and the tips of our ears. Those who tend to become more easily burnt are the fair skinned, blond- or red-haired, the office or home workers who do not usually work out of doors. People like these need to take special care. Even those with the darkest complexion can become burnt if special care is not taken.

When?

The hottest time of the day in any part of the world is usually from 10.00hrs to 14.00hrs. During this period the sun is closest to us and the rays are more penetrating. Likewise, this is the time of the day when many travellers have woken up and wandered down to the pool or beach, and selected their spot for the day. Many will not relinquish their prime spot and struggle on to maintain the territory they have gained. Even taking a dip is marred by fears of invasion so people go for the 'quick in, quick out and back for more sun' method of sunbathing. Such foolishness is often the cause of a spoiled holiday.

Many pools have very little shade or tree-cover close by and so travellers may not realise their extent of sun exposure because of the cooling effects of swimming. However, this shade may also be a natural home to many insects including mosquitoes, so watch out.

Travelling in cars or buses is also another time to take care. Travellers often place their elbow on the window ledge and the passing cool air may take away the realisation that the sun exposure may be intense. Even on cloudy days it is perfectly possible to develop a significant burn. This is especially true if you are indulging in sporting activities such as swimming, skiing or climbing, etc.

Where?

You may become sunburnt anywhere in the world, not just in the tropics. Travellers to the arctic regions or to high altitude frequently become burnt due to the sun's reflection off the snow. In the tropics the sun is more directly overhead and therefore the rays tend to be more powerful; but it is certainly a fact that

more people become sunburnt in the sub-tropical regions — Spain, Portugal, Greece, Italy, etc. — than in the true tropics. Perhaps less care is taken, or travellers to these regions tend to be on shorter holidays and so sunbathe more intensively.

Why?

In our skin we have melanin. It is this substance which takes in the sun's rays and causes the cells to turn a darker shade, giving the appearance of a sun tan. The number of melanin cells in our skin depends on the specific genetic information within each individual which was created at the time of conception: the idea being that if sun exposure is to be more continuous and severe then more melanin is required to protect the individual. Those living in temperate regions where sun exposure is limited generally have less need of the protective effects of melanin.

When travellers visit hot regions, the number and the activity of natural melanin cells may not be sufficient for the intensity of the sunlight. Building up the exposure slowly means that more cells are produced and thus the skin is adequately protected. Unfortunately this takes time and most people are used to demanding instant satisfaction. With regard to natural protection against sunlight this is not possible.

Others, who ethnically have their roots in the hotter regions, have increased numbers of the melanin cells and so naturally have darker skin tones. They are more capable of coping with the sun's rays without serious damage.

Skin cancer

By this stage most travellers will have heard about how sun exposure may cause skin cancer. In some this will only occur after prolonged sun exposure but, unfortunately, in others the effects may be seen after a very limited time.

Different types of skin cancer can occur in association with sun exposure. Some are not that severe and may be dealt with simply by either surgery or radiotherapy. The cure rate for these types of cancer is very high and so perhaps travellers tend, wrongly, not to take this risk very seriously.

Over the past decade or so we have seen an increasing number of patients with skin melanomas in those who have travelled abroad or even got sunburnt at home. This type of cancer is very serious and not always curable. This is the main reason why sun blocking creams and lotions have become big business. What is unfortunate is the fact that some travellers develop malignant melanomas after only very little sun exposure. These tend to be the travellers mentioned above who burn easily. Those with numerous moles are also at greater risk.

What to look out for

If you fit the categories outlined above and you burn easily then follow the suggestions below.

Firstly, know your own body. Learn the normal appearance of any moles you may have had for years. If any mole changes in colour (darker or paler), increases in size, becomes itchy or starts to bleed, then make sure you have it seen to as soon as possible. This probably means as soon as you return home if you are on a short holiday. In between times keep the area covered. Don't get sunburnt.

N.B. It is worth remembering that any mole on a region of friction (bra strap, belt line etc) should be seen and perhaps removed at a convenient time as a protective measure.

Protection advice

All travellers need to take care. If you burn easily then you will need to take all the extra care possible to ensure that your holiday is not spoilt.

- Build up your sun exposure gradually (perhaps 30 minutes extra each day)
- Don't sunbathe over the midday period
- Use light coloured clothing to cover up well. Dark colours attract sunlight and many insects
- Use high factor sun blocking agents at the early part of your trip (start with factor 15 to 25 depending on your

risk, only reduce the factor concentration slowly if you are sure you will not burn. You might only go down as far as factor 15, but do not go lower than 6.)

- Treat any burn areas at an early stage with 'after-sun'
- Drink plenty of fluids (not alcohol)
- Never sunbathe after alcohol
- If you are thinning on top always use a hat when out of doors

People go to the hotter areas of our world to see the sun. The sun is vital for human well-being but, like many other things in life, too much of a good thing can be harmful. Taking simple precautions and using your common sense will help you to protect yourself.

Golden rules

- Never try to get sunburnt
- Cover up well with light, cool clothing
- Use high factor sun blocking agents
- Start with high factor lotions. Work down slowly
- Pay special attention to your ankles, elbows, back of your neck, nose and ear tips
- Use a hat, especially if you are balding
- Drink plenty of clean fluids
- Treat burned areas with after-sun agents
- Never sunbathe after alcohol
- Don't sunbathe between 10.00 hrs and 14.00 hrs
- Tell your doctor if you notice a change in any mole
- Take care against sunburn in buses and on motorbikes

THE RISK OF RABIES

*f*or many travellers the fact that there may be a risk of contracting rabies during their journey comes as a complete shock. Rabies is alive and well in most countries of the world and still causes far too many horrific deaths. International travellers need to protect themselves but many travellers seem to be uninformed as to the actual risks involved; and what they should do if they feel they have been exposed.

Where does rabies transmission occur?

It is easier to say where transmission does not occur. The only free countries throughout the world at the moment include Ireland, England, Australia, some of the smaller Pacific Islands and parts of Scandinavia. Elsewhere transmission of the rabies virus has occurred to humans or the virus has been identified in animal saliva.

How is rabies transmitted?

Rabies is usually transmitted through infected saliva from the bite of a warm-blooded animal. The animals most commonly involved are the dog, cat, monkey, mongoose, raccoon, fox and jackal. In fact, any warm-blooded animal is capable of transmitting the disease. To be on the safe side, if you are bitten by any animal assume that it is warm-blooded.

A bite from an infected animal is the main means of transmission. Nevertheless, there are other ways transmission can occur. Any licking or scratching from an unknown warm-blooded animal must be treated seriously. Never encourage any animal, don't feed them, don't go near them while they are feeding and don't pet animals (they are frequently full of fleas which is another good reason to stay clear).

Children need to be watched very carefully as they tend to wander towards dogs and cats and can very easily disturb them. Discourage your children from going anywhere near animals, especially without your supervision.

Rabies can also be transmitted in another rather unusual way. In the deep caves of Central and South America, the bats may carry rabies and pass the virus out in their urine onto the floor. The virus may then dry into the dust and be breathed into an unsuspecting human. No direct animal contact will have occurred and travellers will be totally unaware of the risk to which they have been exposed. All travellers planning to visit caves in these regions should be vaccinated before their journey.

There is no doubt that dogs and cats are the two biggest animal risks to the traveller. However, any warm-blooded animal may become infected and then may not show signs of the disease for weeks. At this stage the animal is dying and is capable of transmitting the disease to others through its infected saliva. The animals either present in an excited 'mad' phase or in the quieter 'paralytic' stage of the disease.

In the excitable phase the animal (or human for that matter) will suffer severe spasms and will be unable to swallow. Its saliva will ooze out giving the appearance of foaming at the mouth. The inability to swallow saliva is a result of severe spasms and the animal will shy away from any fluids (hydrophobia). Even an air breeze across its throat may set off the spasms (aerophobia). The spasms may also cause the animal to make loud, startling noises. Dogs with rabies can also be seen running around in circles, biting trees, lamp posts, car tyres and showing signs of other strange behaviour. During this excitable phase they may bite many people, an event which occurs most particularly while trying to contain the animal. In general, leave this to the local people who are a lot more experienced.

In the paralytic phase the animal may just appear to be sleeping. Saliva may ooze from its mouth and it may refuse food. In trying to walk, the animal may drag its legs and seem a most pathetic creature. If it is a family pet then, very often, the family will try and force feed the animal and encourage it to take water. This is a very dangerous activity as the family members will have close contact with the animal's saliva and the risk of infection is high. Children often want to care for a sick animal. Don't let them. Leave it to the owners of the animal and encourage them not to force feed the animal but rather to call a vet.

Bear in mind that not all rabid animals go around biting people randomly. Sometimes an animal may seem to have been provoked into biting, giving you no reason to suppose the animal is 'mad'. Don't be fooled — it may still be capable of transmitting rabies. Care is required with all animal contact.

All the symptoms which animals suffer are also exhibited by humans and result in the horrifying symptoms and signs which occur before death. The risk of rabies must be taken seriously at all times when in endemic areas.

When is there a particular risk?

Risk from rabies is highest outside the major cities. This is not to say that an animal bite in the city need not be taken seriously; many of the dogs in the cities are very undernourished and crawling with fleas. They are perfectly capable of contracting rabies and figures from areas like Bombay, in India, estimate that up to 300 deaths occur each year from rabies in the city. However, experience shows that the major time for exposure is when travellers are off the beaten track or staying in small villages. Trekking or jogging are high risk times and you will need to be on special guard.

What should you do if bitten?

As outlined above, the major risk of rabies transmission is from the infected saliva from warm-blooded animals. Obviously, the first precaution is to remove the saliva as quickly as possible to lessen the risk. Wash out the wound with plenty of fluids. Minerals, beer, water, milk — any liquid will do, just wash it out quickly.

Just because the skin may not appear punctured, do not be complacent. Still treat the contact very seriously. After you have washed out the wound with copious amounts of fluids, it may be worth while squeezing gently on the wound edges to see if some blood can be squeezed out easily. Never incise the wound as this may spread the infection. The instrument may also be contaminated. The risk of rabies is bad enough without adding tetanus to the list.

After the initial washing of the wound, rewash the area with plenty of plain water. This washes away any of the soap-type compounds which may have been used, as soap can counteract some antiseptics. Bathe the bite area generously with antiseptic. Cover the wound with a clean dressing and seek medical attention.

If you are not sure where to go check with the local hospital or an English-speaking doctor. If you are completely stuck, contact one of the major embassies in your region. They will always have a contact name for good medical attention.

Nowadays the modern human diploid cell vaccine is always used, either to protect patients before they travel, or to provide adequate vaccination cover after they have been bitten. If you are offered the older Semple vaccine (14 or so injections around the belly-button) try and move urgently to another centre where the newer vaccine is available. The Semple vaccine is made from animal tissue and is more dangerous. However, it still offers some protection if there is no alternative.

How urgent is it to get treatment?

To some extent this depends on whether you have been vaccinat-ed before the exposure occurred. Patients should be encouraged to seek urgent adequate medical attention as soon as possible. Most bites occur on the lower limbs and the incubation time may be weeks or months before the first symptoms commence. If the bite occurs on the upper limbs or side of the face then the incuba-tion period may be shortened to just a few days. This is the most serious area to be bitten and it is imperative to get medical atten-tion as soon as possible. The incu-bation period is dependent on the distance the site of the wound is from the brain. A bite on the ankle may seem minor, but it is impor-tant to get further vaccination cover, even if this means putting an early end to your holiday.

Should you be vaccinated before your trip?

Obviously it is impossible to gen-eralise. Some people live in the tropics for many years and never see an animal with rabies, while others get off the plane and are bitten within the first week. So who should be vaccinated before they travel?

In general, a six month period is used as rule of thumb. Anyone planning to live for more than six months in a region where rabies occurs should consider vaccination. Also those planning to trek out of the major cities in Africa, Central and South America, India, Nepal or many of the other regions in Asia will be at higher risk. Those planning a caving trip in South America will also risk exposure. Any traveller specifically planning to have animal contact, e.g. vets, will also be in a higher-risk category.

The vaccination is fairly expensive but it is easy to give, works very well and has few significant side-effects.

Conclusion

Never disregard any bite, lick or scratch from any warm-blooded animal. Always treat them very seriously. Watch your children very carefully and discourage them from playing with any animals overseas. Never smuggle any animal back home. The animal may appear perfectly well for months but still be harbouring the deadly rabies virus.

If bitten:
- Wash out the wound with any fluid
- Apply an antiseptic
- Look for competent medical attention immediately
- Have rabies vaccination before your holiday if you plan to trek, or you will be living in risk areas for more than six months. Remember children are at special risk because they usually love animals
- Never befriend any stray animals
- If an animal is sick, call a vet. Don't try to force feed the animal

SPIDERS AND SCORPIONS

Snakes

Snakes are found all over the world and travellers and locals alike are naturally terrified of being bitten. In fact, death from a snake bite is very uncommon; it is estimated that less than 10% of those bitten will die. In addition, tourists are seldom bitten, and indeed, it is quite possible to live all one's life in the tropics and never encounter a single snake.

Snakes tend to avoid human contact and will quickly move away if allowed. The danger occurs when humans are unaware of their presence and accidentally threaten them. Accidents can be minimised for travellers if they are aware of snakes potential hiding places. Carrying a torch when plodding around in the dark is also highly recommended.

Snakes are generally grouped into four categories, no fangs (not dangerous), back fangs, front fangs and folding fangs. The venom is designed for immobilising small prey and not for killing humans. Consequently, an encounter with a human often spells disaster for the snake. Most bites result from an accidental encounter where the snake will bite quickly and then try to escape. This rapid exposure usually means that no venom has been injected and the risk to health is negligible. Small snakes move away when approached, larger ones depend upon camouflage and will hiss to warn you to halt. Some snakes, e.g. black mambas, are territorial and will defend their area. Black mambas are dangerous and have a tendency to hide in houses and store rooms.

Pet dogs, and particularly cats, are excellent snake detectors. After heavy rains both snakes and spiders may be flushed out of their holes. However, most bites are not lethal and needless medical complications can be precipitated by sheer panic.

The only antidote to venomous bites is a serum prepara-

tion. The use of a tourniquet has always been controversial and is probably best avoided. Also, the practice of cutting or sucking the bite of the wound has little to offer; you may even cause tetanus or blood poisoning.

The shock of being bitten alone can cause breathing difficulties and it is vital therefore for both the victim and the helper to remain calm. The vast majority of people will recover gradually from snake bites. However, it is important to try and get expert help quickly, and, if possible, to try and identify the type of snake. If the snake can be safely killed, bring it along for identification purposes.

Don't forget that there are also sea snakes, and, although their bites are not painful, their venom affects both muscle and tissue. Fortunately their poison is slower-acting than land snakes and there is usually time to get emergency help elsewhere.

Spiders

There are over thirty thousand species of spiders living at altitudes ranging from sea level to sixteen thousand feet, so it would be difficult not to encounter them at some time during your travels. All of them have venom glands but only a few, e.g. black widows and brown spiders, are harmful to man. Again fear and panic after a bite is responsible for many of the medical problems related to spider bites. The spider has much more to fear from you than you have from it. Be very careful putting your hand into dark hidden spaces.

If bitten, using painkillers like paracetamol and a cold compress is all that is required under most circumstances.

Scorpions

About eight hundred species of scorpions exist. Most are nocturnal, but again, heavy rains can flush them out of their habitat at any time. There are two generally poisonous types: one which is relatively harmless to humans and the other which may occasionally cause death. They will usually retreat rather than attack and therefore contact with humans is always accidental. The ankle beads and jingles worn by many local people in tropical rural areas around the world are designed mainly to cause noise when out walking so as to warn off snakes, spiders and scorpions.

Adults will seldom die following a scorpion sting but children may be badly affected. Be very careful if out late in the evenings, especially if it is a moonless night.

PROBLEMS WITH ALTITUDE

many travellers think of a holiday as a chance to lie on a beach. For others, a holiday means getting out into the open spaces and climbing hills or mountains. Those who are well experienced in climbing may not find this a problem but for others it can be a very different story.

It is essential to recognise that air becomes thinner at higher altitudes. This means that there is less oxygen available and the result is that we need to breathe more rapidly or more deeply in order for a sufficient supply to reach our lungs. Under normal circumstances, we tend to slow our activities, lessening our oxygen requirements and thus only breathing relatively normally.

However, climbers tend to over-exert themselves. They want to push on to their goal and certainly they do not wish to be seen by others as being unable to cope. The early signs of altitude sickness are commonly disregarded and so serious consequences can easily occur.

These early signs may be masked by various factors until the climber is relatively quickly overtaken by serious symptoms. One of the highest risk times is overnight while the rest of the party is sleeping. The sufferer may slip into gradually deepening unconsciousness and by the following morning an emergency situation could well have arisen.

So, are there any precautions which should be taken before the holiday? When are travellers particularly at risk? What are the main symptoms and signs of altitude sickness? And what should be done?

Before departure

Certainly if you are planning a holiday which will require you to climb to heights above about 7,000 feet it is wise to check that your body will cope. The main two areas of the body which are affected are the cardiac and the cerebral systems.

Knowing that you are in good shape is at least a start. Have a medical check and make sure that your doctor knows you intend climbing during your holiday. Know the altitude you hope to reach. Your doctor will pay special attention to your heart, blood pressure, pulse and lungs. If you have a history of significant asthma, angina, hypertension, diabetes or migraine then special care will need to be taken. Don't go on a climbing holiday if you are pregnant.

If your doctor advises you against undertaking a high altitude climb then listen to the advice. It is given for your protection.

Where and when are the risks?

As mentioned, most of the risks regarding altitude sickness occur while climbing over 7,000 feet. The symptoms and signs may even be noticed at lower levels and this is especially true if the traveller is suddenly deposited from a pressurised plane at levels much higher than they are used to. These can be even as low as 4,000 or 5,000 feet, especially in those getting on in years and with a history of heart disease.

One of the times when travellers can experience real problems is when flying into Ecuador or Nepal. They suddenly find themselves at high altitude where the air is very thin. Their breathing becomes a bit laboured but they don't want to slow down the party, so they say nothing. That traveller is aiming for trouble. Real difficulties can occur and the problems are not worth the risk.

One thing to watch is the unanticipated climb. This often happens on holidays when travellers see a bargain trip and stupidly forget the basic rules regarding higher altitudes. Holiday makers to Nepal who anticipate trekking should likewise take extra special care.

Symptoms and signs

Symptoms are what you feel. Signs are what others can find while examining you.

In climbers the main symptoms and signs of altitude sickness include the following: dull headache, tiredness and lassitude, shortness of breath, chest pains, difficulty in focusing, dizziness, swelling of the ankles, irritability and poor sleep pattern. Any of the above would be a cause for concern and care should be taken to deal with the situation as soon as possible.

What should be done?

Firstly, once any of the symptoms or signs become evident, don't dream of going any higher. You should wait at that altitude until you settle. If settling does not occur within a short period of time, then descend by at least 500 feet. Even this small descent can be life-saving and certainly the symptoms should decrease.

Only return to your ascent after you have settled fully for at least 24 hours. Most of the serious consequences associated with altitude sickness (and don't forget this includes death) tend to occur in very healthy young males who don't want to appear 'weak' and so struggle on to show their prowess.

Medication to lessen the effects of altitude may occasionally be recommended. Remember, all the problems associated with altitude sickness are because the body is telling you something. It is your body's

PROBLEMS WITH ALTITUDE

way of ordering you to give it oxygen. Drugs tend to fool the body into being able to go on regardless. If you slow your activities or descend to where there is a more plentiful supply of oxygen, then all should be well. Take care with the use of painkillers while climbing as they may mask the early warning symptoms of a headache.

One of the most dangerous times is during sleep. If you have any symptoms, tell a responsible fellow traveller before you retire for the night. A useful rule to remember is: climb high during the day, so long as you descend to sleep at night. This gives you the best of both worlds and will help to keep you safe.

Conclusion

Climbing brings a new realisation of the wonders of our world. Just take care, follow the basic guidelines and look out for each other.

Golden rules

- Before you leave, know your itinerary and the altitude you hope to attain
- Have a medical check-up and inform your doctor how much and how high you intend to climb
- Start to get fit
- Always climb slowly
- If any symptoms of altitude sickness occur, descend by at least 500 feet
- Climb high during the day, but make sure you descend for sleeping — remember

106

that night time is one of the more dangerous periods

- If you have symptoms, admit them and don't struggle on

Symptoms usually include:

- Dull headache, tiredness and lassitude
- Shortness of breath
- Chest pains, vision problems
- Dizziness, swelling of the ankles
- Irritability, poor sleep pattern

A selection of altitudes (in feet)

Alice Springs	1,901
Aswan	366
Athens	351
Baghdad	111
Bombay	37
Cairo	381
Cape Town	56
Caracas	3,418
Colombo	24
Delhi	714
Dodoma	3,675
Geneva	1,329
Hong Kong	109
Istanbul	59
Jerusalem	2,485
Johannesburg	5,463
Kathmandu	4,344
Kampala	4,304
Khartoum	1,279
Lagos	10
Lima	394
Livingstone	3,161
Majorca	75
Mexico City	7,575
Nairobi	5,971
Quito	9,350
Rio	201
Singapore	33
Sydney	138

THE

T
TREKKING
HOLIDAY

rekking holidays have become more popular over the past few years. At times, however, travellers may suddenly decide to wander off the beaten track at short notice and it is then that they will usually be ill prepared.

Some of the commonest areas where holiday makers undertake trekking holidays include Nepal, Thailand, India and parts of central America. Treks in Africa tend to be mammoth affairs and attract many travellers each year. In many of these regions trekkers are very well catered for and so there is no great difficulty in obtaining adequate supplies of

food and water and good hotel/hostel accommodation.

Before your trek

Ask yourself the following questions. Are you really healthy enough for the trip? Do you like to walk? Have you ever walked as far as you plan to on this journey? Make sure you don't take on too much. None of this macho stuff! Just realise your own limitations, stay within the boundaries and all should be well.

During your trip

Trekkers do face some special risks and will need to take care if they are to stay well.

Food and water problems

Most of the major problems associated with food and water are covered in their own chapters. Nevertheless, trekkers will need to take extra care. Frequently after a hard day's walk, almost any food or water will be thought acceptable. Your level of care will be diminished and suddenly you may find yourself facing days of illness. This is especially true when you are tired and your own common sense may not be up to par. Consider buying a good portable water filter before you leave.

Bites and stings

If you are out walking in the rural areas it is more likely that you will be faced with mosquitoes, sandflies, snakes, scorpions, dogs, cats and any number of other animals. Make sure that you are well clothed and that you have a sufficient supply of insect repellent to last until you reach the

next large town. The chapters on bites, stings and rabies cover the major points which need to be considered. Make sure that you always have a good torch close by and try to stay on the main paths. Be very careful if you wander off into the bush looking for water or a place to pitch your tent. Take your time and don't walk under any overhanging trees or bushes which are a favourite haunt for snakes.

Clothing

Make certain you have good boots which cover your ankles, one of the commonest areas to be bitten or stung while out walking. If you are travelling for days, have enough washable clothing. Always give clothing and bedclothes a good shake and make sure to look inside your shoes before you put them on.

Be careful if you can't iron your clothes. In many of the tropical areas, certain flies lay eggs on damp clothing. When you next wear the clothes, the larva may burrow under your skin. They are not particularly dangerous, but the thought of a larva under your skin is enough to turn even the strongest stomach! The solution is to hang your clothes to dry in a screened area or to iron all your clothes before you wear them. This includes socks, babies nappies, etc. Always sleep on a raised platform and not directly on the ground. Try and set up a mosquito net if you are sleeping outside.

Trains, planes, buses and boats

We have already covered jet lag resulting from long plane journeys. The physiological effects of high speed jet travel, which brings your physical body to a new time zone before your biological clock has had time to adapt, is one of the prices we pay for progress.

This effect is not as noticeable when travelling on long journeys by boat, train or bus. Nevertheless, those modes of travel carry with them their own particular disasters and delights. The delights are self evident; time to acclimatise, to relax, a chance to view the scenery and a better opportunity to meet local people. The disasters include motion sickness, boredom, time delays, higher risk of accidents and food- or water-borne infections. For those travelling in developing countries, it is essential that they have their itineraries well planned in advance, if at all possible.

Boat journeys in particular are potentially very dangerous. There is the ever-present risk of overcrowded boats. If the boat looks unsafe, think about waiting for another, or taking alternative transport.

Travelling long journeys by bus in the tropics can be even more hazardous. Apart from the appalling road antics of talented tropical bus drivers (who can sleep, eat and drink at the same time as driving) the vehicles themselves are often held together by an extraordinary range of odd parts. It is amazing to see how much can be packed into (and onto) a passenger bus. Whole families, and sometimes their entire house contents, accompany the bus traveller. On these journeys a good source of food is any fruit which can be peeled, boiled eggs and properly-sealed sodas for drinks. These can be bought without leaving your seat (or your luggage) through the bus window at any of the many local stops along the way.

One word of caution: thieves! The common denominator noted on all continents is that the thief is usually overdressed in a poncho-like garment, which leaves the hands free to work on your valuables.

Finally, one of the greatest health hazards encountered while travelling by local transport is the ever present risk of infectious disease as a result of spitting, coughing, sneezing, vomit or indeed lice-borne disease from close physical contact. Perhaps the best advice is to minimise your use of local transport and use instead only means of transport which have been recommended for tourists.

After the journey

Remember that you have been exposed to more potential illness than many 'normal' tourists. Your very lifestyle will have placed you in a higher-risk category. Watch out for any signs and symptoms which might suggest that you have been infected.

Attend your doctor and explain that you have recently returned from abroad. Describe your living conditions while overseas. Don't forget that signs and symptoms of illness may not present for days, weeks, months or, occasionally, years after your trip.

ENTERTAINMENT BORNE DISEASE

You may be asking yourself what items could possibly be covered in this section. The truth is, the international traveller is exposed to many kinds of disease, some of which need to be addressed with sensitivity.

Holidays are for enjoyment, a chance to break the routine which has been set throughout the year. During this break, the traveller may may forget many of the safeguards which are designed to keep us healthy.

Walks, exercise, sports, good food and the night-life: all of these often represent a change from everyday life for the traveller. A number of people will have accidents while abroad. The numbers vary but estimates suggest that between 0.1% to 1% will have an accident which will affect the remainder of their journey adversely. Road accidents in particular are a major cause for concern among travellers. Keep your eyes fully open as you cross the roads and constantly check which way the traffic is coming from.

If you plan to engage in water sports, check the look of the centre before you pay any money. If the area is dirty, looks uncared for and has obviously rusty equipment, think twice before you take part. Look for the presence of life-guards and check if your travel insurance covers you during water sport activity.

The twisted ankle is a common, but not too serious, cause for concern due to night-life activity. Often, the dance floors are crowded, the alcohol consumption has been excessive and the need to prove oneself too great. Watch out.

It would be difficult, in this section, not to mention the problems associated with casual sexual contact while overseas. The whole realm of sexually-transmitted disease is closely linked to entertainment, and this is never more true than when overseas. Defences are down, alcohol is up, normal protective values disappear and opportunities arise: a lethal combination.

There are three main groups at high risk:

The business traveller

Imagine the situation: a businessman has flown across many time zones for a four day set of meetings. On the final day, a deal is struck to the satisfaction of everyone. The businessman will fly home on the first flight the next morning, and that evening is

spent enjoying a good celebratory meal, some wine and a well-deserved rest. Perhaps he will have a few extra drinks, enjoy some rather pleasant company and, when he wakes up the next morning, the pleasant company he picked up the previous night may have left him with more than he bargained for.

The tourist

A similar situation but, perhaps, more time is available and with it the chance of more exposures. There may have been only one single 'contact', or many. Still, infection could have happened on the first occasion.

The sex tourist

Don't be fooled — this can be a male or female tourist. They go to an area with the specific intention of engaging in sexual activity while abroad. Females, actually, have a higher risk of contracting disease. This form of 'tourism' is very big business in some countries. The 'tourist' in this category will look for the younger contact, thinking the risk of HIV infection may be somewhat lower. These 'tourists' may be better prepared than those having casual contact, but they are a very high risk group, especially as they return to their own home country.

The risk is not just from the AIDS virus; other very serious diseases are transmitted in this fashion. These include syphilis, gonorrhoea, hepatitis B, herpes virus and many more. Condoms do not offer full protection. The quality of many condoms manufactured in developing countries may not only be very poor, but they also may not be easily available.

The seriousness of this whole situation cannot be over-emphasised. Don't underestimate your ability to get into serious trouble. If you have already been through a similar experience, contact your doctor and discuss the facts thor-

oughly so that your own health, and that of others at home, may be safeguarded. Remember that the AIDS virus can also be transmitted through contaminated blood or infected needles. Never have a blood transfusion unless there is no other choice. Never plan to have dentistry while in a developing country and don't have your ears pierced or acupuncture while abroad. The risk is just too high.

The motto 'experiment, but with care' is not true in the area of sexually-transmitted disease. The risks are not worth the benefit. If there had to be a bottom line on this whole topic it would read — DON'T.

Note

Some of the vaccines may be contraindicated in individuals with an altered immune status, e.g. AIDS patients or those on steroid medication. There are various possibilities open, but this needs to be discussed in depth with your doctor.

HOW TO TREAT

*i*n this short book, it is obviously not possible to turn each traveller into a fully qualified doctor, able to deal with every situation which may arise during a trip overseas.

Nevertheless, it is important that the traveller is able to recognise illness, assess its severity and commence treatment as and when necessary. Very often this early treatment will solve the problem and further intervention may not be required.

These are some of the more commonly faced problems.

Treating diarrhoea

Two important things to check are that there is no blood present in the diarrhoea and that there is no high fever (usually greater than 38°C/102°F). If either of these are present, medical attention should always be sought as soon as possible.

If the diarrhoea seems to be a more straightforward case of 'Delhi belly' then the use of one of the common anti-diarrhoeal medications is probably all that is required. If the diarrhoea is persistent, or you are passing more than two stool motions each hour, then watch out for dehydration.

Take small amounts of clear, clean fluids frequently. Don't gulp down large quantities of liquid. Abstain from alcohol. Perhaps give food a miss for 24 hours, but clear soups and a very light diet should be safe. Don't plan any coach trips until you are properly back on your feet.

Treating sunburn

Sunburn is the same as a first- or second-degree burn caused by hot metal or boiling water. It needs to be treated in the same way and the severity will depend on the extent of the area involved.

Firstly, control the pain with paracetamol. Cool the affected area with after-burn creams. Wear loose, light-coloured clothing and be very careful of the regions where friction might occur. Lie down for a while — adequate rest is very important.

Extensive sunburn can be serious. Again, look out for dehydration and make sure that a sufficient fluid intake is maintained. Patients often complain of a dull, throbbing headache but paracetamol will usually control the major symptoms.

Lukewarm baths, once you can get under the water, are marvellous at providing instant relief. Showers tend to be too painful unless they are very gentle.

Be especially careful not to get sunburnt a second time in the same area. Use plenty of protective, high-factor creams and wear a wide-brimmed hat and sensible clothing.

Treating fever

Firstly you need to identify that there is actually a fever and that it is not just the ambient temperature. Use the thermometer which should have been carefully packed in your first aid kit.

The chapter on medical attention overseas outlines some of the reasons why fever is an important sign of illness within the body. A raised temperature certainly always needs to be taken seriously, especially in children.

Ensure a good intake of fluid so that dehydration is avoided. If there is any sign of neck stiffness, or a skin rash, medical attention should be sought. If you have

packed antibiotics, don't take them without medical advice unless the situation is very serious and no competent medical attention is available.

Travellers often feel that fever must be a sign of malaria. It is perfectly possible — if the time of exposure has been in excess of one or two weeks. Before this time, fever is frequently caused by simple colds and influenza. Make sure you have packed 'your' remedy for the common cold before you leave home.

Treating diarrhoea, nausea and vomiting

This combination is a common occurrence while overseas. Usually you will be able to trace the cause to an apparently mild indiscretion at a meal some hours previously.

The combination of diarrhoea, nausea and vomiting frequently leads to dehydration. Watch out for the characteristic signs and try and replace fluids as soon as possible. Don't rush them in, you will just vomit all the more. Sipping a spoon of clean water every five minutes or so will get a large amount of fluid in without much discomfort.

Anti-nausea tablets, or syrup, may also be helpful. Again, take it slowly, don't try to gulp it. Lie down, dim the lights, try and relax. Take slow, deep breaths in through your nose, hold it for a few seconds and then let it out through your mouth. Some of the acupressure bracelets seem to offer good help to many travellers.

Note

If you do require medical help, be careful about allowing the doctor to give you any injections. Watch to see if the syringes and needles are in sterile wrapping. Only have an injection if there is no other alternative and if you feel everything is sterile.

The vast majority of international travellers will have no particular problems while abroad — just think before you act.

MEDICAL

ATTENTION
OVERSEAS

*n*o matter how carefully you follow the rules, sometimes you just get sick. If the illness is fairly mild, the items in your first aid kit will come in very useful.

If, however, you suffer any of the following you will need to look for medical attention.

Significant headache, especially with neck stiffness

A pounding headache may occur in association with dehydration, over-exercise, consumption of alcohol, following an accident or from an infection.

Profuse diarrhoea or vomiting

Up to 30% of travellers will devel-op some type of diarrhoea. In a small proportion the diarrhoea will be significant and they will require further therapy. Look for signs of dehydration: dry tongue, dry palms, thirst, sunken eyes, lethargy and muscle pains or cramps.

Diarrhoea with blood or fever

Always check any diarrhoea for the presence of blood (dysentery). This signifies a deeper infection and will always require further treatment. Fever is also an important sign and must never be disregarded. Check it with your thermometer, don't just feel the forehead.

Skin rash

The biggest organ we have is our skin. Frequently a sign of internal disease will show in the form of a rash. If you develop a rash, take a picture — it may help to make a diagnosis at a later date.

These are probably the biggest areas of concern which will drive the traveller towards finding medical attention while they are overseas. If you have a holiday representative, ask them for help. If you are travelling on a less organised journey, ask for advice from the hotel or hostel management. Usually they will be very helpful and will point you towards a local doctor or the nearest hospital.

If all else fails, look for the nearest embassy or consulate. You will find that they will be slow to offer assistance unless the situation is very severe. They get so many calls from ill-prepared travellers that they only act as a final resort. Nevertheless, if the situation is severe they will certainly help you out where possible. Try and obtain the names and phone numbers of English-speaking doctors in your area, especially if you plan to wander. In that case, make sure that you have an adequate first aid kit. In many of the developing countries the locally available drugs may be out of date or not well prepared and therefore less effective. Carry some of the more important ones for your journey as they may be of great value, either to you or the doctor for your treatment.

travel in health

—

Section 3

After You Return

AFTER

YOU RETURN

you have returned from your holiday. You had a marvellous time. Everything ran smoothly and you were delighted with the choice you made. You followed the rules and stayed healthy. Is there anything that you should do at this stage so that your next trip will also run smoothly?

Alternatively, perhaps you were one of the less fortunate travellers who just seemed to get sick, no matter what. Is there anything you can do now to ensure that you regain your health as soon as possible?

What to look out for

It would be quite easy to become paranoid and then assume that every single cold, muscle ache or mild headache means that you have come home laden with a multitude of rather nasty, foreign parasites.

The majority of international travellers stay healthy, return home and continue to remain in perfect health following their journey. Nevertheless, it is important to realise that your journey will have brought you to areas where serious illnesses may be different to those at home.

Also, the incubation time may be very long — certainly weeks, if not months. Very occasionally, years may pass before you develop significant signs or symptoms. However, this is rare, so there is no need to panic.

Firstly, if you are one of the very few who does feel ill after returning home, symptoms will probably have occurred within the first one to two months. After this the chance that a foreign bug is involved is possible but becomes less likely. The typical symptoms and signs which should make you attend a doctor include fever, headache, influenza symptoms, skin rash, diarrhoea, nausea and vomiting, significant lethargy and muscle aches and pains.

Your symptoms may be unrelated to your trip but your doctor will be able to put your mind at rest. Never struggle on by yourself fighting unusual symptoms. It may be that there is a simple remedy and your doctor will be able to advise you best.

The medical check

Not every traveller will require a medical check after their journey. Some, however, will feel they have nothing wrong with them and yet they will still benefit from a post-exposure medical check-up. These are usually travellers who have lived overseas for a long period of time or those who know they have been exposed to disease while abroad, typically trekkers.

The doctor will need to know the answers to some or all of the following questions:

*   Where were you while abroad?
*   For how long?
*   Did you take your malaria prophylaxis, if required?

- What vaccines did you have before your journey?
- How many were in your party?
- Were others sick?
- Did you eat local foods? What types specifically?
- Did you use tap water?
- Where did you swim?
- Did you get sunburnt?
- Were you bitten by mosquitoes? Or by any other insect?
- Were you bitten by a dog/cat/monkey, etc?

After this background information your doctor will review your time abroad. You need to be able to relate any episode of illness which occurred and what was done about it. Did you have medical attention? What did it involve?

Your past medical history, along with that of your family, will then be briefly reviewed. Your doctor will also want to examine you to see if there are any signs of swollen glands, chest infection, enlargement of the liver or spleen and various other specific tests depending on your history. Following this, the doctor will probably request various investigations. This will frequently include a blood screen and also tests of your stool and urine. Even if you have no symptoms, these tests are worthwhile. Up to 30% of long term travellers have evidence of being exposed to parasites. The vast majority of these are harmless and will require no treatment.

It is vital to realise that even though you may have had a full post-exposure medical screening with the doctor, you still can develop signs and symptoms, even for the first time, some months later. This would be unusual, but it is possible. Just remember to keep an open mind and don't forget you have been abroad.

Your next trip

Most international travellers continue to travel. Once you have experienced the real joys involved in seeing new cultures, experiencing different cuisines and meeting and making friends, it is difficult not to travel again. So, accepting that you probably will venture abroad in the future, should you do anything at this stage to prepare? Absolutely. Some simple actions now will save hours of frustration and heartache for the future.

Safely pack away your passport and your vaccination card. Choose a place where you will remember them for your next journey. Check the expiry date of your passport, and if necessary, make a note in your diary to renew it in plenty of time.

Before you hide away your vaccination card, check if you were advised to have a final vaccination after your trip. This is very common if there was not sufficient time before your departure. If you do need a final vaccination, note the date and make an appointment.

Sort out your foreign money. Keep the various currencies separate but in the same general area.

Make notes on what you enjoyed, and also what went wrong on this trip. Put the list with your travel documents and plan to review it before you book your next holiday. Give marks out of ten to the travel agency, the resort and the time of year. Once all of that has been organised, you can look forward with confidence to your next trip abroad.

ACKNOWLEDGEMENTS

*i*t is not possible to write any book without the assistance of a number of people. These nameless folk are essential but nevertheless receive little credit. We would like to give our grateful thanks to those who have helped us.

Our wives and families

Without the constant support, endless cups of coffee and general encouragement, 'Travel in Health' would have remained a dream. We can never say how much we both appreciate our families. Medical schedules and constant trips overseas and various projects have meant Sylvia and Terri have had to cope with the homes during these times. Thank-you.

Medical and technical information

The final responsibility for the information contained in 'Travel in Health' must rest with its authors. Much of the advice is based on our own personal experience from our trips overseas during the past 20 years. Nevertheless we gratefully appreciate the marvellous assistance offered by various groups including the World Health Organisation.

It is impossible to be certain that the hard-fact information remains correct continually. This is especially true for the pages relating to the countries reporting yellow fever, cholera and malaria. If you are planning to visit any of these areas it is vital that current information is sought. Appropriate action should then be taken to protect yourself.